Will Grega's

GAY MUSIC GUIDE

Pop Front Press   **1994**

The GAY MUSIC GUIDE is published by Pop Front Press,
147 Second Avenue #498, New York City, NY 10003
Phone (212) 777-7240

The inclusion, mention or photograph of any individual or group herein or on the Sampler is not necessarily meant to infer or imply anyone's sexuality, sexual practices, or sexual preferences, homosexual or otherwise.

Will Grega's photo by Sunny Bak. Please see individual albums for artist photo credits. All material on the **Gay Music Sampler** is copyrighted. Please see individual albums for copyright information.

Printed and manufactured in the USA.

Library of Congress Catalog Card Number 93-87452

Thanks to: Randy Jones, Michael Callen, John Turner, George Coeminskie, Jimmy Rodriguez, Patrick Arena, Sunny Bak, Mark Bego, Paul Corrigan, Quentin Crisp, Mitch Gallob, Jan Brady, Jack Godby, Grant King, Dan Martin, Michael Biello, John Orlando, OutMusic, Paul Phillips, Doug Rose, Joseph Victor Sieger, Doug Stevens, Bert Wylen, Jon Arterton, Reno, Bert Herrman at Alamo Square, Cathy Andrews at Goldenrod Horizon, BookCrafters, DiscMakers, Matthew Sartwell at Publishing Triangle, Frances Green and Howard Smith at GAYELLOW PAGES, and Marge Barton......RJ and I would like to thank our wonderful families, and my angel (I love you, Gramma!)

And special thanks to Arthur R. Armstrong, founder and conductor of the Metropolitan Gay & Lesbian Orchestra

DEDICATION

Dedicated in loving memory to Michael Callen, a man who made a difference. Thank you Michael, for your generosity of spirit and support for this project. You will always be the spirit of gay music, and the very best of us.

...and to the talented men and women
in the **GAY MUSIC GUIDE**:
you *are* the music of our lives!

INTRODUCTION

Music is magic in many people's lives; it sets a mood, speaks for the collective subconscious, soothes, seduces, arouses, and serves as the soundtrack for our lives. Music is a bridge to ourselves, a starting point, the portal to bliss. Music unites us and sneaks into the tiniest cracks of the American superculture. To pop culture junkies of all taste levels, music is just more drugs—experience enhancement. Folkies have spread populist political messages through music that have inspired everyday man to forever change the destiny of this country. Music is everywhere in the world around us; in our homes and cars, restaurants and shops, all popular forms of entertainment from TV to films and video games. Stars are shot up the *Billboard* charts in a weekly drama that involves positions and bullets, managed personas, and strategically manipulated images. The multi-billion-dollar-a-year music business congratulates itself with alarming redundancy: *The Grammy Awards, The Billboard Awards, The American Music Awards, American Country Music Awards, People's Choice Awards* and on and on. We have powerful memories associated with popular tunes and with the music we loved through the days and times of our lives. Music has expanded consciousness, set trends, and has introduced language into the popular culture. Music has made us think, cry, fall in love, laugh, shout and scowl. Music enthralls, distracts, attracts detractors and ardent supporters. More cultural information is passed through the pop music form than through all the information in books and magazines combined; and music information makes its point quicker and with greater repetition. Pop music stands head-to-toe with film and TV as the biggest cultural influence of our time. And in the increasingly fractured multi-cultural American present, it was only a matter of time before music with gay and lesbian messages found its way into gay and lesbian lives.

That time is now. In fact, 80% of the albums listed in the **GAY MUSIC GUIDE** were recorded in the past four years (the Gay 90's)!

We hear a lot in the gay and mainstream media about (established superstars) like Elton John, Melissa Etheredge and k.d. lang, and how brave they are to have come out of the closet. Yes, they have taken bold steps and deserve our praise.

But I think it takes a lot more integrity for an artist who is just beginning a career to say, "I'm gay and I write about gay issues," and to invest thousands of dollars of their own money in their own record companies and products (cassettes and CD's).

On the integrity scale, there is no comparison. These are the artists who deserve our support. I was thrilled to have discovered the Gay Pop Music explosion, and I'm sure you will share the thrill of discovery that awaits you in these pages and on the **Gay Music Sampler**. I encourage you to take an active role in the dissemination of gay and lesbian culture by ordering the releases you hear and read about that strike your fancy. You can ensure the survival and growth of this most fledgling of the gay cultural arts with your orders.

Market research shows that gay and lesbian people buy eight times as many cassettes and CD's as the average consumer. We have a unique historical opportunity to use our significant economic clout to send a message to the entertainment industry: we support music with a specifically gay perspective... the music of our lives!

If you have not already done so, turn to the back of the book and order your Free **GAY MUSIC SAMPLER**, a 24-song, 90-minute Sampler of many of the best gay and lesbian music artists you will be reading about. In the text, the "loudspeaker" symbol indicates that the artist is featured on the **SAMPLER**.

Note: Many of the releases you will read about are available at your local gay, lesbian, feminist and new age bookstores. For your convenience, I have listed information (boxed) within each review where you can order these releases directly from the artists. When you order, make checks payable to the name or company that appears in **bold type** in the first line of the box. CS is the code for cassette format. CD, of course, is for CD format. LP refers to vinyl releases. If an 800 number is listed, I would strongly encourage you to order by telephone. In cases in which you would like to order multiple items from any one performer, you will most likely be able to get a price break on postage. Also, and this is important, **all prices listed include postage.**

Shipping charges are included in the listed prices!

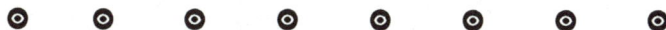

◉   ◉   ◉   ◉   ◉   ◉   ◉   ◉

...AND LEЅBIAN

For the purpose of brevity, when I use the phrase "gay" in the text, it is intended to encompass lesbians, bisexuals and any other alternative sexualities that wish be included. One of the benefits of taking on this project was a renewed appreciation for my lesbian sisters, many of whom I now consider friends. Thanks to all the women that this project brought me in contact with!

MARGIE ADAM: NAKED KEYS (1980)

Instrumental piano. There is an intimacy that exists between Margie Adam and the piano that is sensuous and playful, and her 1980 release allows us to peep at these performances from outside her window. Yet there is something oddly sexy and very gratifying about that, even though she doesn't invite us into the action. The eleven keyboard pieces, done in *George Winston* fashion, showcase a wide range of emotion that radiate Margie Adam's warmth and human spirit. There's a determined moodiness and inner reflectiveness to this album and, coupled with chunky chord styling, that puts her squarely in *George Shearing* territory. The compositions are played as picture postcards rather than stories without words. Titles include: "Woodland," "Seahorse," "Resting Place," and "Waves." Sensitive, passionate, ethereal and bold, if this is Margie Adam "naked," take it off, honey, take it *all* off!

MARGIE ADAM: ANOTHER PLACE (1993)

Pop. From the mid-seventies to the present, Margie Adam has helped define and expand the notions about Women's Music as an art form, a political force and an industry. Back then she was one of The Big Four in Women's Music. (The others were *Holly Near, Cris Williamson,* and *Meg Christian*). Together these Women's Music pioneers created an alternative music scene that sold millions of records. This is her first vocal album after a seven year hiatus, and is an incredible return to form. Margie Adam has a classically American traditional writing style with verses and bridges that musically surprise and choruses that lift these remarkable mini-movies toward pop heaven. The arrangements are cool, jazzy, breezy, and deeply felt. With a voice like a summer morning, you gladly go the places she's leading and it's well worth the trip. Achingly romantic and lovingly political, this album is an unqualified quiet storm winner. Wistful melodies call to mind *Pippin-*era *Stephen Schwartz* or top-of-her-

> **Pleiades Records**
> PO Box 7217
> Berkeley, CA 94707
> *NAKED KEYS*: CS $12...CD $17
> *ANOTHER PLACE*: CS $12...CD $17

form *Carole King*. Margie Adam touches nerves that open up a wide range of feelings—the full sweep, in fact: from poignant gentleness to foot-stomping celebration, from deep sorrow to grand exaltation. Her trademark orchestral piano style has a vibrancy and drama that draws from classic Broadway musicals while blending the influence of *Gershwin* and Brazilian rhythms. Her rich alto voice evokes *Anne Murray, Joan Baez,* and *Janis Ian. Another Place* is moving, sweet and easy to listen to; it insinuates itself into your heart and is impossible to shake. This is a gentle gem of an album.

What impact would you hope your music has on other people's lives? I hope my music speaks beyond my experience as a woman or as a lesbian. It's certainly my intention to have my music accessible to everybody.

ADULT CHILDREN OF HETEROSEXUALS: ADULT CHILDREN OF HETEROSEXUALS (1993)

Rock/cabaret. Very scary stuff from an outlandish mix of gay and lesbian performance artists in Boston who probably spent a little too much time at the midnight screenings of *The Rocky Horror Picture Show* (in full costume drag). The four songs on this theatrical release are: "I'm So Hard So I'm So Easy," "I Never Liked You Anyway," (which is a read up, down and in every direction!), "I Wanna Get Married," and "It's Risky!" The music, which tends toward the raucous, blends avant-garde jazz, cheezy synths, sax, and vocal ensemble around male and female featured vocalists. As ACOH romps about smashing stereotypes and bending genders, the results run from the pointedly amusing to the screamingly hilarious. Part of Boston's *Theatre Offensive* and founded by members of the legendary *United Fruit Company*, this hard-edged, co-gender cabaret band is guaranteed to entertain, provoke and excite with their blend of high camp and low humor. Brazen and hard, you would not want to run into any one of this troupe in a darkened alley. ACOH pushes the envelope, but first they stuff it and give it a good lick!

Will McMillan
8 Westwood Road
Somerville, MA 02143-1518
ADULT CHILDREN OF HETEROSEXUALS: CS $7

D.C. ANDERSON: FOOL MOON (1990)

Vocal/Jazz. D.C Anderson is simply the most accomplished romantic balladeer of our community. He is a veteran of LA's *Phantom Of The Opera* company, and has toured nationally in *Nicholas Nickleby* and *Pippin.* Last year, Anderson produced the 2-CD set, *Cabaret Noel: A Broadway Cares Christmas,* which featured such luminaries as *Tommy Tune, Amanda McBroom, Scott Bakula, Karen Akers* and others. His two solo albums on the Lockett Palmer label make up an arrestingly moving body of work. In fact, these are a pair of albums of unparalleled beauty. Breathtaking performances and an exquisite repetoire of standards and startling and uniformly charming new discoveries make these sets a dream. A constant delight, you will find yourself coming back to these albums time and again. On *Fool Moon,* he lends his beautiful tenor to a diverse collection of songs by *Stephen Sondheim, Duke Ellington, James Taylor, Enya, Johnny Mercer, Rupert Holmes, Leonard Cohen* and *Carly Simon.* Heartwarming and heartbreaking, Anderson's interpretations are moving without being melodramatic, and he projects an easy charm and warmth that is positively cuddly. His reading of "No One Is Alone" (from *Into The Woods*) is worth the price of admission by itself. Songs of hope and humor ("If I Only Had A Brain," "I'm Beginning To See The Light") round out the album and tie nicely into the theme. If you've ever been a fool for love (every time?), D.C. is your man.

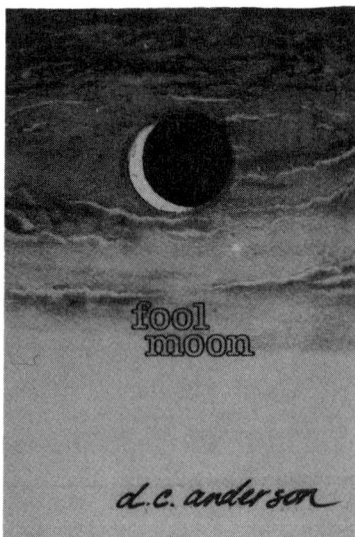

> **Lockett Palmer Recordings**
> PO Box 85557
> Los Angeles, CA 90072
> *FOOL MOON:* CS $12.50
> *TIME WAS:* CD $17.50

D.C. ANDERSON: TIME WAS (1993)

Vocal/Jazz. Ear candy for incurable romantics, this album will sit comfortably on the shelf beside your *Tony Bennett* and *Michael Feinstein* collections. Highlights on this heartfelt collection are "That Night," "I'll Follow My Secret Heart," and "A Cock-eyed Optimist/The Great Peace March Medley." With cello, bass and guitar added to the stirring piano playing of *Lem Jay Ignacio,* the playful arrangements complement the gentle and surprising D.C. Anderson readings. This album is an unqualified delight from start to finish.

What has been your musical path or journey? My musical tastes are eclectic:

D.C. Anderson

TIME WAS

songs from the theatre, folk, jazz. I like to sing with a piano, an acoustic guitar and bass. I love a cello and voice together. Music has its own path to my heart. I have certain issues that come up again and again in the songs I choose to sing: love and responsibility, care for children, the struggle I have giving into and alternatively giving up romantic fantasy, family life. I hope people who listen to what I sing get to know themselves a bit better by doing so.

What is gay and lesbian music in your definition? Any music a gay woman or man is creating or listening to at the time.

What do you think is the future of gay pop music? My vision is that I do not have to go to the back of the store to a Men's or Women's Music section to find voices that sing of love for members of their own sex. I think that is the future.

ROBIN ANDERSON: INVERNESS (1993)

Folk/pop. Robin Anderson was born during a thunderstorm under auxiliary power, which could explain the influence of energy and the elements in her music. We feel her pain, her anger, her gathering strength. The project (alternatively charming, chilling, strident, and humorous) is dedicated to survivors, and addicts and alcoholics in recovery everywhere. Anderson possesses a commanding voice, and sings from the depths of renewal. The full guitar sound and her powerful voice combine into a rich compound that transcends notes and lyrics. She is a person who has dredged the depths of her pain for art, and bolsters and illumines us all; and the sincere desire to share the emotion behind it all is expressed through each song. If you like the *Indigo Girls*, you will genuinely appreciate the work of this incredible woman.

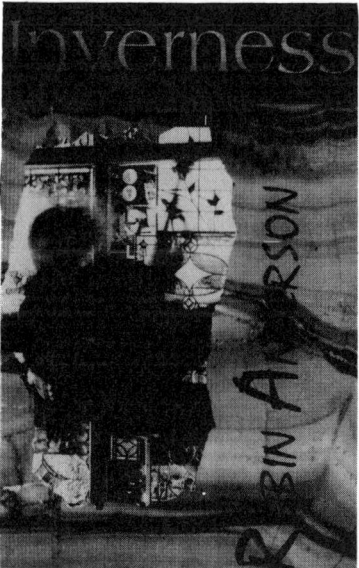

How do you hope your music would impact people? I've been moved, inspired, saved, and emboldened with the music I've had in my life. I

Robin Anderson
4632 Shenandoah, #2 West
St. Louis, MO 63110
INVERNESS: CS $12

want people to hear some piece of my perspective in my music. I want my heart and my hands, my worn shoes, and little scraps of me hanging in my music. The possibility that my music could rejuvenate, heal, challenge and follow people throughout their lives is part of my craft.

TINA BENEZ: GLAMOUR OVERDOSE (1993)

Rock/pop. Born to be a pop goddess, Tina Benez delivers one of the most wildly orginal EP's of the 90's! "Hitler's Daughter (High Fascist Model)" is a chilling peep into the fascistic (but highly fashionable) future of the world politic. "Glamour Overdose (G.O.D.)" is a scream from start to finish, and is delivered over a highly polished Eurodance/rock track. The vocal samples and overall production are brilliant and tasty. Included on this four-song set of originals is "Ghost In You," a phenomenal ballad with an arrangement reminiscent of *Ennio Morricone's* spaghetti Western film scores. If Tina Benez wants to take over the airwaves, I am all for world domination of Hitler's daughter!

How would you describe what you do? Drag n' Roll, Nunu Wave, Pink Rock, Andro-Glam, Pansexual Pop. Tina Benez is the gayest! What's it like being Tina Benez? So gay it hurts!

How has music impacted your life? Music hits me like a Mack truck, and is my greatest escape.

What is your definition of gay music? Boring! I make good music, regardless of who I'm sleeping with. If I was straight, my music would still be genius, just with different marketing. Yes, we all market ourselves every day; that's why it's called the human *race*.

Why have you chosen to do gay music? Is there really any other choice more glamorous, more carefree, more happy? I think not!

What is your vision of gay music? Farsighted. I live very much in the pop future. I think we are going to have two sides of the coin: on one side, very conventional pop, and on the other, total anarchy. I love flipping coins!

RICHARD BONE: QUIRKWORK (1992)

Alternative dance/pop. A founding member of NYC's electronic music scene, Richard Bone started his career by writing music for off-Broadway theatre productions (using home-made processors), and has worked with neo-legendaries *Lenny Kaye* and *Reeves Gabrels*. In 1980, he joined *Shox Lumania*, but soon went solo and released a string of singles on Chrysalis Records. He has produced singles for *Rubber Rodeo*, composed original music for award-winning cable and broadcast television, and has been involved in the music video production of his own work released on the experimental Sony "Video 45's" in the early 80's. On *Quirkwork*, tricky arpeggiated passages, layered vocals and deft production combine to make these dance-floor friendly tracks a real treat. Bone creates pop/dance hooks with a 90's sensibility, and well knows his way around a recording studio. Tracks include: "Last Days Of Heaven," "Calling All Cars," and "Eveready Strut." Dark, sexy dance music and light, dancy sex music with influences ranging from *The Beatles* to *Roxy Music* and *U2* merge to create a quirky pop delight.

How do you define gay music? With the exception of those fine artists who try to make a difference with "gay issue" music, I like to hope that gay music would be human music with unlimited appeal. But, I do not write gay music. I am a musician who happens to be gay. I don't spend my time being an out musician, although if asked I will gladly answer questions about my sexuality. However, I assure you my next CD will not be titled *Dance Of The Really Pink Triangles*.

> **Quirkworks**
> PO Box 229
> Greenville, RI 02828
> *QUIRKWORK*: CD $12.99

What is the future of the gay pop genre? I hope gay artists will continue to create works of universal appeal and prove once and for all that we are all members of the human family.

JOE MACK BOYD: THAT I COULD STILL GO FREE (1993)

Contemporary Christian. How could anything bad be said about an ex-convict turned Minister of the Gospel of Jesus named Joe Mack Boyd who writes songs with titles like "Jesus Signed My Pardon"? Especially when the man runs a gay church

> **God's Growth Garden Center**
> 20509 Highway 79
> Sleepy Hollow #16
> San Jacinto, CA 92583
> *THAT I COULD STILL GO FREE*: CS $7

"*That I could still go free*"

and a homeless shelter for men who are HIV positive. While he is still refining his vocal style, there is no doubt that Boyd has found the spirit. A former inmate who spent four years behind bars until Jesus "settled me down and set me free," Joe Mack Boyd describes himself as "a 32-year-old curly-headed blue-eyed 200 pound 6'1 inch southern boy from Louisiana who just enjoys getting on with the business of living life to its very fullest." His album features a cover of the now-classic *Marsha Stevens* (see listing) song, "For Those Tears I Died." Salvation for a song.

What do you hope to accomplish as a gay gospel artist? My goals are to sing for as long as I have breath and continue to share the good news that Jesus loves you no matter where you are, what you've done, or what people may tell you to the contrair'.

JOE BRACCO: TRUE TO MYSELF (1992)

Pop. Joe Bracco represented one of the best hopes for gay music's future when he sadly died of AIDS in March of 1991 at 30 years of age. But thanks to *Paul Phillips* of *Romanovsky & Phillips* (see

JOE BRACCO

True To Myself

listing), Bracco's buoyant performances live on. *Phillips* took a collection of the late Bracco's rough home recordings and demos and layered them with lush instrumental arrangement enhancements to create a wonderful posthumous tribute to a true pop talent. The collection sparkles with Bracco's warm personality, melodic pop/New Wave influence and true gift for lyric writing. That Bracco is gone is a real loss for our community, though his music will live on in this tape of his most affecting material. "Friend In My Pocket" is a goofy tribute to condom-use; "I Don't Like To Say Goodbye" is touching and sad, but tough; "Window Whacker" needs no explanation. These recordings are proof that Joe Bracco was a rare and compelling talent (a New Wave *Bruce Springsteen*) and *Paul Phillips* is to be commended for bringing Bracco's

Fresh Fruit Records
369 Montezuma #209
Santa Fe, NM 87501
1-800-473-7848
TRUE TO MYSELF: CS $13

superlative gift to light for the whole community to discover. An upbeat and enjoyable tribute to a talented and courageous man with New York attitude!

BUTT BOY: FEEL THE MUSIC (1993)

Techno/ambient/leather. Thrust Recordings specializes in music written expressly as sensuous sounds for those serious about leather. This sensual music has the mellowness of New Age, the orchestral influence of classical music, the sharp edge of rock, and the futuristic sounds of techno pop, with a heavy leaning toward early *Pink Floyd* and the synthesized electronic pop of *Jean-Michel Jarre.* Already an accomplished composer in video, radio and theatre, *Butt Boy* brings his sexual music into the private places of the leather community's play places and sets the mood required for a mind trip into the erotic. "Dance Of The Whip" builds its swirling sound around the rhythmic pattern of a cracking whip. The thumping beat and all-male chant, "Depths Of All Pleasure" bows to the distant melody of "3 a.m." This is a tape that should come with *protection*!

What is Butt Boy all about? I write music to put gays in the mood for sex. Each piece of music was written to be an enhancement to the gay erotic encounter. I write music to help gays free their inhibitions about their sexuality. **How has music impacted your life?** Music impacts me the same way it impacts everyone. The difference with me is that I am conscious of what's happening to my psyche when music is playing and most non-musicians are not. Music is like liquid emotion that flows out of the speakers and onto the listener, saturating them into feeling that emotion. My goal is to put a feeling that I feel into a recording and then let the recording work its psychological power on the listener, making them feel and think what I want them to. With this subconscious method of manipulation, I can put the listener into an erotic mood or a party mood within minutes of listening to my music. There's this long-distance relationship that is unspoken between the listener and myself as they experience my music. People who want to be put in the mood will want to put in my tape. **How do you define gay and lesbian music?** I don't think there should be "gay and lesbian music." Music is its own purpose. Artists

Thrust Recordings
PO Box 29212
Dallas, TX 75229
FEEL THE MUSIC: CS $18

should be liked and disliked for the art they put out, and not judged because of their sexual preferences. But, since society insists on seeing us as gay musicians, I like to consider myself to be "extra gay" over other gay musicians, because my music has been composed to be played during the very activity that marks us as gay: same-sex intercourse.

Why have you chosen to compose gay music? A composer's music is supposed to be an outward expression of his or her inward feelings, regardless of how society feels about those inward feelings. This "forbidden" sexuality is a strong feeling inside me. And as an artist, I say, "Here it is. As it is. In an unashamed musical expression."

How do you envision gay music's future? I visualize gay music being accepted for its worth. Not being liked because it's a Novelty Music, but truly being liked because the musicians and composers are just damn good at what they do.

MICHAEL CALLEN: PURPLE HEART (1988)

Rock/pop/vocal. Leading AIDS activist Michael Callen single-handedly redefined the public's concept of a person with AIDS after his diagnosis with the disease in 1982 by giving speeches, writing articles, appearing on national television, giving interviews, organizing within the community, campaigning, and singing at a tempo that would exhaust most healthy people. His political efforts have been chronicled in *Randy Shilts'* classic book, *And The Band Played On.* His musical output is nothing less than amazing, and includes recording two albums as one of *The Flirtations* (see listing). His debut solo release was recorded six years after Michael was diagnosed with HIV, had established the PWA Coalition and testified at Congressional hearings on AIDS. *Purple Heart* is nothing less than the most stunning gay album recorded to date.

> **Significant Other, Inc.**
> PO Box 1545
> Canal Street Station
> New York, NY 10013
> *PURPLE HEART*: CS $12...CD $17...LP $10

The album has a pop/rocking set that segues into a more intimate set of six songs with Michael at the piano, and contains the classics "Living In Wartime," "Love Don't Need A Reason," and Callen's ultra-campy reading of "Where The Boys Are." This amazingly affirming album sets the standard by which all gay albums will be judged for years to come. It is a must-have by an outstanding human being and hero to our community with one of the most wondrous voices ever recorded, and about whom Elizabeth Taylor said, "His life is a shining symbol of hope, strength and courage." His impact will be felt on this community for years to come.

MICHAEL CALLEN UP CLOSE

(This interview was conducted with Michael Callen shortly before his death in December of 1993. At the time of his passing, he was furiously at work putting the finishing touches on *Legacy*, the album he realized would be his last. The multiple-CD set is scheduled to be released late in 1994).

Describe your music and what you do in your own words as an out gay person. I sing and write about my own experiences, and my favorite art is art that comes from the specific truth of an experience. As an openly gay man, and as a man with AIDS, I couldn't imagine any other way of writing songs which didn't deal with being gay in a deeply homophobic society. At this late stage in my life, people tell me it's radical and courageous, but it's really laziness, because I can't imagine any other way of writing. I find it absolutely astounding that the experiences of 5-10% of any given population never, ever are heard in any kind of mainstream way. We gay people are constantly expected to be able to translate the divas ("Oh, my man I love him so...") into our own experiences, and I think straight people are perfectly capable of translating gay to straight. If I'm singing about loving another man, they should just sort of say: How is that like what I feel...gee, that's *exactly* like what I feel! It's the emotion that is universal. I'm a

MICHAEL CALLEN

big fan of the details and the specifics, and there are gay cultural references that sometimes make my songs less acceptable to uneducated or unsophisticated straight people. It isn't my intent to cut them out, I'm just not interested in concealing who I am, and since I am a gay man, often my songs reflect that experience.

Is it important to reach out to mainstream America? I crossed that bridge a long, long time ago. I think anybody that tells you they wouldn't like to be rich and famous is lying to you. My friend *Cris Williamson*, who I adore, has taken a lot of heat because she doesn't feel she writes "Women's Music" only for women. She writes as a woman hoping that there is some universal truth that men *and* women can learn from and enjoy. A lot of people used to say that was a cop-out, but I definitely have come around to her way of thinking. You have to make the best art you can make and put it out there, and it will have a life of its own. Your art will speak to straight people or it won't. I don't believe in pulling any punches; I don't censor, afraid people might miss the references in my lyrics. Other artists make different choices.

Where did you come from? What was your upbringing and education? I am an escaped convict from the bowels of the midwest. I think of myself as poor white trailer trash. But I've noticed that every third homosexual comes from the midwest, one of those "I" states. I'm from Indiana. I was raised in a very religious environment, a very small town called Rising Sun, where I was a sissy and tortured and tormented until I was able to escape to go to college and discover my people. It's been a lifetime of healing. And for me, making art and singing about that process has been very healing. And I've been lucky enough and honored enough in my life that people have written me and said that some of my songs have helped heal them also.

Who would you name as your personal artistic influences? Well, I would say without question that my three major influences are: *Elton John, Barbra Streisand* and *Bette Midler*.

What has been your artistic path or journey to get where you are today? Well, I'm going to have to make a bunch of embarrassing admissions, but after you've gone on *Donahue* and said you've had 3,000 men up your butt...really, you forfeit all rights to embarrassment.

This is the truth. Nobody believes it, but you'll just have to take my word for it. Singing for me publicly has always been torture. I have loathed every second of it. Touring with *The Flirtations* finally beat it out of me. Performing night after night and feeling the waves of love finally cured me.

I inherited from my poor father (the subject of "Nobody's Fool"), this absolutely impossible perfectionist system of judgment, and I was constantly judging each and every note I sang: was this the best note I could have possible have sung? Did I sing it perfectly? Did I hold it long enough? Was it perfectly in tune? Did the vibrato come in at exactly the right moment? And that's really not what singing is about. Only this last year, something about dying has caused a continental shift in my perspective, and I finally discovered what has been underneath all of that, which is joy. And I have been making *Legacy* mining this deep vein of joy that's been there all along, and it has been the greatest, happiest, most artistically fulfilling time of my life. Every single song that I sing, I love! I've written about forty percent of the album, and the remainder of the songs are by friends or are cover tunes that I've loved all my life and sung all my life. And even though my lungs are three-quarters karposi's, and I haven't been feeling all that well, it's very strange, and I'm an atheist, but *the spirit descends when I sing.* I'm always exhausted and limp after this channeling. But when the tape starts and I'm singing a song that I love, you wouldn't know that I was sick until the song ends and I collapse. I am so alive in those moments, and it's a little sad for me to realize that if I would have just gotten over myself and taken myself a little less seriously all those years, I could have had a steady diet of this joy. But it has to do with classic gay low self-esteem: I have to prove my worth, I must be perfect, I must be the best little boy in the world. There was no harsher audience than the little voice inside me saying: you're shit, you're nothing, you're not a singer, who are you fooling?

And yet you have the greatest gift of the most amazing talent that is the envy and awe of all your peers. I'm glad you've found that joy. I am too! When I start to get sad thinking about how much time I wasted, my boyfriend points out to me that some people die without *ever* having had a taste of it. I have at least had nine months of it.

There are those who say that I had a white bread or a "Wonderbread" voice and that I could have been a *Barry Manilow* if I'd really aggressively pursued it, and sung romantic ballads with the "she" pronoun. I would have loved to have had his fame, his money, his gold records, but I got right up to the moment where I had to sing "she" and I just couldn't envision it. I don't have any experience of having romantic love for "she's." So, my immediate response when I starting out was to do something a lot of gay people in my generation did: I went through what I call my "second person" phase. I scoured the music library for songs that were gender non-specific and constructed this whole elaborate defense: Oh, it's more universal, let the reader fill in...

Gradually, I realized that was a cop-out and I was spending a lot of energy avoiding singing my truth, "he." It didn't take me long to take that leap. And whether or not I was foreclosing any possibility of commercial success, I guess we'll never know, but I haven't regretted it at all. So far, we don't have any examples of someone being openly gay first and becoming a successful commercial artist. Somebody's going to do it, though.

What was the artistic path that led to your recording career? I was a child soprano prodigy. I was a boy soprano. I realized I had a voice at an early age, a *soprano* voice. Then that got beaten out of me because beyond a certain age, boys are not supposed to sing soprano.

My first musical influence was *Julie Andrews, "To Laugh With A Delicate Air."* You can imagine the poor scenes with my father, as a I sang that song with a British accent. It was just not done.

Much later, in New York, I sang at *Snafu* and the *Duplex* and the whole circuit, kind of half-heartedly. Singing was agony for me, and I would throw up before a performance or lose my voice because I was tense, and I loathed every second of it. And the most frustrating thing during that time was that everybody used to assume that I was having the time of my life and that singing was the most natural, easy thing in the world for me. They would compliment me on my natural voice, while I felt like I was pushing a piano through a transom. If they only knew...

And then the AIDS war came. My favorite myth these days is Cincinnatus, who only wanted to be a farmer but was called away from his plow to lead the Roman army to keep Rome from being destroyed. If I hadn't been so involved in the AIDS political struggle, I would have made a lot more art. I was constantly making agonizing choices between singing/performing and giving a speech or giving testimony or chairing a board meeting.

Purple Heart came about due to my then boyfriend, *Richard Dworkin*. I give him complete credit. I got sick and it looked really grim and he basically said: If we make it through this, I think it would be an absolute scandal if you didn't leave the world some record of your music. So, I did recover and he agreed to spend our money and undertook to produce *Purple Heart*, which I thought would be a one-shot deal. I thought no-one would buy it because I wasn't prepared to tour. I wasn't well enough to tour, and that's really the only way you sell an independent album. And it really did drop like a stone. Very few people heard about it.

Over time, however, that changed. The people who have heard *Purple Heart* **hold it up as the hallmark against which all gay albums should be judged.** I'm very proud of it, although *Legacy* is an order of magnitude beyond *Purple Heart*. It's just the best thing I've ever done. I think the difference is joy, but I've also had the good fortune to work with some of the best artists in the world who have been so generous to drop what they were doing to come and make this possible.

Do you think it is important for gay music to be taken to mainstream American via the big record companies? Yes. That's the equivalent of the "color line." We'll know the revolution is near when that happens. Times are changing and somebody is going to take that leap of faith starting a career as an out gay artist, and it's going to work commercially. But I think it's hard to convince emerging artists that that strategy is likely to pay off. Unfortunately as of this date, you can't name a major label who has signed an openly gay artist (at least in America). The British scene is different.

You got involved with The Flirtations in 1988. How did you go from full-blown musical arrangements and a solo career to becoming a member of an a cappella group? Well, there's an interesting story that I told at my final concert in Washington at the *1993 March on Washington*. I was a closeted soprano. I had been literally made fun of and smacked for singing like a girl, and I just happened to have these incredible pipes, only I was embarrassed about it. No one really knew. I was a tenor, so I sang high anyway, but nobody had ever heard my soprano. I met *Richard Dworkin* in the summer of 1981 and we moved in together and one time I was in the kitchen singing along to the radio in my best soprano, and he came running in and said, "What was that?" and I got all embarrassed and admitted it was me.

Richard slowly convinced me to expose my talent to the world. We were in a lesbian and gay rock band at the time called *Lowlife*, so he insisted that I sing more and more lead parts. I was horrified, waiting for people to shoot me or start laughing. It was really Richard and his love and support that has enabled me to be proud of that part of my voice.

I was also so busy and so stressed out with AIDS activism that I missed *The Flirtation* notice in the *Village Voice*. Richard caught it and made an audition appointment without ever telling me—in Brooklyn. "What? I don't go to Brooklyn!" And he told me it was an audition for an a cappella group and that it was perfect for me and I moaned and pissed and resisted. But I went and the rest is history...gay history...herstory. The *Village Voice* certainly does bring people together: it's how I met my lover, it's how I met *Pam Brandt*...and *The Flirtations* ad changed my life.

What is gay and lesbian music in your definition? I think the notion of a gay community is a necessary fiction. I don't think there is one, but I would say that it's really useful and wonderful to pretend that there is, and to act as if there is.

Gay and lesbian music is simply music made by gay and lesbian people, or music specifically about the experience of being lesbian or gay.

What is your vision of gay music? Where are we going and how far? How much of an impact can we have on the 90's? Will gay music cross over to the mainstream and is that important? I think there's a step missing, an important step. Our heroic lesbian sisters have created something called Women's Music, which of course really was Lesbian Women's Music. They built from scratch an audience, a distribution network, and recording labels owned and controlled by women. They produced a cultural phenomenon where women supported women artists. There is absolutely no gay male equivalent of that at all, and I would say that before we talk about crossing over to the mainstream, we have to go through that community-building stage. The average gay man doesn't begin to know what gay music is or who the "stars" of gay music even are. Hopefully, the GAY MUSIC GUIDE will help change all that.

The women *are* ready for mainstream success, because they have a demonstrated track record. *Holly Near* has sold something like two million albums in her lifetime. Any record company is going to sit up and take notice of figures like that. *Cris Williamson* has sold nearly a million albums. That's the way I think you break into the industry: you prove to them that it's in their financial interest and that there is a market, a loyal following that will buy these albums. Gay men need to do their homework. If the gay community, and gay men in particular, support gay music, the results are going to be amazing for music and for the movement.

KEITH CHRISTOPHER: KEITH CHRISTOPHER (1993)

Pop/rock/soul. An exceptionally talented vocalist with a wide range and a personable, embraceable quality, Keith Christopher produces music that is melodic, endearing and just plain thrilling to hear. His songs reflect the emotions and issues of today in a style that is strong and vulnerable, passionate and clear. He has composed special material for *The United Nations Environmental Program* as well as *The Names Project.* Christopher sings about love and loss with unbridled hope for a better world. Sublime and gratifying songs reinforce his belief in the power of love as a force for personal growth and physical health. The tracks on this debut are muscular, lush, with hip 90's rhythms that surround his made-for-radio, big white soul voice. Christopher himself is a tall, blond god with soap opera star looks and a strong tenor. He has the power, control and purity of *Kenny Loggins*, and the sexy white Motown growl of a *Michael MacDonald* or *George Michael.* The uptempo tracks will have you moving and grooving, and "Smiling In The Dark" will have you swooning. In a world too often separated by differences, Keith Christopher's music is about what unites us.

What's it like being an out gay performer? Being an out performer makes life a hell of a lot simpler. I've learned that you can't be counted unless you are willing to stand up.

What do you hope will be the impact of your music? Music lifts us up and inspires us. It comforts us in our pain. It makes us dance and it makes us cry. Music seduces us. And that's why songwriting is a responsibility as well as a gift. It's the opportunity to seduce people into listening to what you have to say, maybe even considering a larger viewpoint about life and our world. I hope that is what my work might accomplish.

> **Keith Christopher**
> KCT Productions
> 230 Riverside Drive #14F
> New York, NY 10025
> *KEITH CHRISTOPHER*: CS $10

How do you define gay music? Gay/lesbian music is a statement of personal power. It's about celebrating our freedom from society's ideas about how we should love or live or express ourselves. The splendid value of the GAY MUSIC GUIDE is that it provides our community greater accessibility to its own voice and passion.

What is your vision of gay music? I see gay music as an expression of a larger consciousness and power growing in our community. Gays and lesbians all over the world are saying to the rest of humanity that we must be recognized, that we count, our lives count, our deaths count, our dollars certainly count, and every other part of our being here, including our music, makes a difference.

DAVID & JANE: DAVID & JANE...NOT ASHAMED (1993)

Gospel/pop. David & Jane is a unique combination of a gay man and lesbian woman singing gospel music who tour full-time around the country making a living pursuing music careers! They are vanguards in the use of inclusive language, a testimony to their belief in God's love for everyone. Both David and Jane are ministers based in the greater New York City area, and they have been featured at *New York City Gay Pride Festivals* since 1991. Jane Syftestad received her formal training at UCLA and the prestigious *Manhattan School of Music.* David Heid, who is currently on staff at the renowned *Julliard School*, also serves as the Music Director for the *Metropolitan Community Church of New York.* This is jump up on your chair and wave your hands and say hallelujah kind of fun, with first-rate originals ("Standing On The Promises." "Bless It Back," "Rejoice") and stirring covers ("My God Is Real" and "Farther Along"). A collection of glorious songs that only goes to prove that God *is* on our side!

What's it like being gay/lesbian gospel ministers? Being gay performers is exciting and rewarding. We draw from our diverse backgrounds in traditional gospel and contemporary Christian music to create what we hope is a unique sound and ministry. Certainly the *Hawkins Family* and *Sandi Patti* were

---

David & Jane
304 East 38th Street, #2C
New York, NY 10016
DAVID & JANE...NOT ASHAMED: CS $11

early influences. Still, people find it shocking to be at a religious service/concert and see two people talking about their lives in open, honest ways. But audiences can be touched more deeply that way.

What has been the impact of music on your lives? Music has really defined both our lives. It is our passion, our calling, our destiny in life. All the doors for us keep opening in that direction. There are so few people in our field that are, through music, telling people they are okay in God's sight. We often feel that if we don't say it, it's not going to get said in the way we want it said. It is our hope that people who hear us are changed by what they hear.

What do you think is the future of gay pop music? Our vision for the gay community is to reach everyone who wants to hear with positive, supportive messages and images. So much of people's identity in the 90's is defined by pop culture, media, etc. that it is vital that we exist in this area to give our people positive identification.

DAVID DIAMOND: QOWBOY (1993)

New country. A legend while still in his teens for being a founding member of *Berlin* ("The Metro," "Sex I'm A...") and racking up numerous gold records, David Diamond discovered that country music was what really saddled his

horse. He's a fine producer and writer, gifted with a voice that sounds remarkably like *Don Henley* of *The Eagles*, and evokes the whole Southern California country sound of the late seventies. Delivered with intelligence and solid pop smarts with sliide gee-tar and California country/rock thrown into the stew, this radio-ready cassette is a pure country/pop confection by a superb stylist. Diamond balances the release with good time songs of the *Highway 101* honky-tonk variety, and cryin' in your beer numbers. The fragile, whispery delivery of "What I Need" is the dream/nightmare of a broken man, and is the chilling, open-a-vein country style perfected by *Roseanne Cash*. Diamond explores the pain of a shattered soul loving too well, losing and bruising: hard stuff that goes down smooth. Ride 'em, qowboy!

How did you get from *Berlin* to country music? I spent a good portion of my life hating country music. When asked about my musical preferences, I would often cite country music as the exception to my liking pretty much all types of music. I changed. What I looked for in music changed. And country changed.

I needed substance from the music I listened to. I needed to be told a story which I could relate to and believe. I needed to hear the honesty that had become so clearly absent from pop music. Much to the horror of many of my longtime friends, I found what I was looking for in country music, so this tape is not my attempt at country, this is my commitment to country. I wasn't raised in Nashville, I never worked on a farm, I didn't marry my high-school sweetheart and I don't drive a pick-up truck. But I came very close to losing my dog, I've lost many friends to the plague of the era, I've had my heart broken, and I keep my eyes open to the world. I used to feel that country music was about living in the south, getting drunk, and getting into fights. I thought it was for narrow-minded rednecks who hated folks like me. I feel differently now. To me, country music is a musical expression of what it is to be honest, sensitive and coping; a celebration of the human experience.

And these are things I know very well.

Who are some of your influences? Growing up I listened to *Elton John, Aerosmith* and *David Bowie*. I loved *Elton* for his bravery and his sensitivity to music, *Aerosmith* because they were so raw yet tasteful, and *Bowie* because he was the

| David Diamond |
| 2 Butch 4 U Productions |
| 1427 Sanborn Avenue |
| Silverlake, CA 90027 |
| *QOWBOY*: CS $10 |

first proof I ever saw that being different was in fact better. Country artists have been more of an inspiration than a direct influence: *Dwight Yoakam, Clint Black, Garth Brooks.*

Why have you chosen to do gay music? I don't do gay music. I simply do music and happen to be gay. I certainly don't see what I'm doing as an alternative to a mainstream career. I have no choice but to do what I do. It's who I am. Assuming that gay music does indeed exist, I see it's future going in the direction of New Wave. Once people get over the newness of it, it becomes so mainstream that its difference becomes invisible.

DIAMOND ROSE: THIS ROAD CALLED LIFE (1992)

Folk. With rare honesty and haunting melodies, Diamond Rose writes from the heart. This is an entertaining blend of styles: JayDee is bluesy and playful, Steven Gellman is woeful and bummed; this presents a compelling mix in this diverse acoustic duo. Gellman plays a handmade stringed instrument that has become a trademark of the Diamond Rose sound. The "strumstick," a

DIAMOND ROSE

THIS ROAD CALLED LIFE

cross between a banjo, mandolin and dulcimer, is unique in sound and appearance. Gellman's voice, like his lyrics, is powerful and sensitive, and the group's lyrics consistently achieve a delicate balance between humor and poignancy, while the hypnotic chord changes evoke a *REM*-like dreaminess. JayDee's lyrics are laugh out loud hysterical, and her voice brings to mind *10,000 Maniac's Natalie Merchant*; at times fragile, at times sardonic and playful, it is a voice that captures both the depth and whimsy of her lyrics. The romantic obsessions of Gellman remind us how fragile we all our in our hearts; he writes of loss and longing. Future outings plan to mine the dreamy writing qualities of this group with full studio production and more of a rock band sound. A promising premier by future killers, Diamond Rose are seriously committed performers who will challenge your perceptions of acoustic music.

Diamond Rose
PO Box 0077
Rockville, MD 20848
THIS ROAD CALLED LIFE: CS $8

How has music impacted your lives?
JAYDEE: Music makes life worth living.
STEVEN: I couldn't go a day without hearing music. We hope people will feel the emotion and honesty in our songs, and maybe someone somewhere will say, "That's *my* song; that song was written for me, that's just how I feel."
How would you define gay and lesbian music? Our opinion is that there is no gay/lesbian or straight music. There's just music. There *is* music performed by gay and lesbian performers, and that is probably the most beautiful and sensitive music. We've simply chosen to pursue music careers, and not hide our sexual orientations.

ALIX DOBKIN: LOVE & POLITICS, A 30 YEAR SAGA (1993)
Folk/pop. Proto-punk and militant lesbian Alix Dobkin has been pushing people's buttons for years and God bless her for it! Until recently a vocal separatist, we men are fortunate she's come around to sharing her talent with us. Dobkin first started breaking down barriers with her now-classic debut, *Lavender Jane Love Women* in 1973 (the first internationally distributed lesbian album ever), and after twenty years she is still one of the few blatant lesbians in Women's Music. (She has twice been voted "Most Popular All-Time Performer" by *Hot Wire Magazine*'s Reader's Poll). This collection is a compilation drawing from her five albums, plus a couple of previously unreleased tunes. It is a fine and

representative sampler of one woman's work centered around what Dobkin considers the two most important forces in most lesbian's lives: love and politics. The 20-song work traces her career chronologically, and highlights many of the songs which have established her as a leading proponent as well as a foremother of contemporary lesbian culture (included are "Amazon ABC" and "Lesbian Code"). Her music is full of humor and

> **Ladyslipper Music**
> Dept B.
> PO Box 3124
> Durham, NC 27715
> 1-800-634-6044
> *LOVE & POLITICS, A 30 YEAR SAGA*: CS $16...CD $19

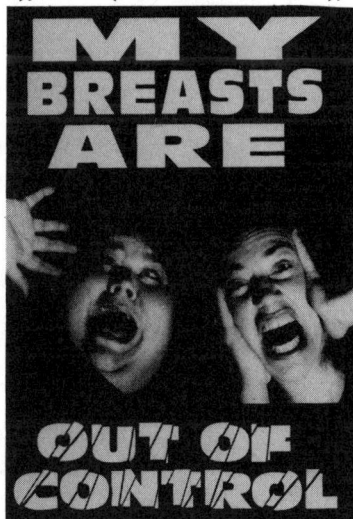

compassion, and burns with the fire of struggle for equality and the celebration of difference. This disc establishes the greatness that is Alix Dobkin and is a vital document of the genius of a lesbian legend.

How do you describe your music? I write songs and sing material supportive of women in general, lesbians in general, and always promoting common strengths and good sense.

What has been the impact of music on your life? Music has always been in the forefront of my life; having been raised in a musical family, it has been one of our strongest bonds and values. Music gives us joy, inspiration and enlightenment, and I hope my music does the same for others.

And the future? Lesbians will always have our own music, but probably not pop. As for me, I am incapable of existence in the mainstream, so there is no choice for me but to continue doing what I'm doing.

Who do you listen to? *K.T. Oslin* (any album), *labas* (Brazilian drummers), *Phranc* (*Folksinger, I Enjoy Being A Girl*).

DOS FALLOPIA: MY BREASTS ARE OUT OF CONTROL (1992)

Comedy/musical parody. Dos Fallopia is an outrageous kamikaze comedy duo combining music, sketch comedy, razor sharp wit, left-wing politics and general lunacy. *Lisa Koch* (see listing) is the funniest and most prolific songwriter/comedienne on the scene today. Teamed with *Peggy Platt*, a renowned stand-up comic and actress, the pair do a non-stop, two-woman assault and trouncing of all things sacredly lesbian and feminist. Warning: This album sets its sights on anyone who takes herself too seriously. Dos

Fallopia trashes wimmyn's music festivals *(Dolphin Free Tuna Woman* and *Compost Morning Dew* sing highlights from *My Uturus Sings)*, 12-step day care clinics, *The Judds* ("Singing Backup For Jesus" and "My Dog

> **Tongueinchic Productions**
> 1202 E. Pike, #712
> Seattle, WA 98122
> *MY BREASTS ARE OUT OF CONTROL*: CS $12

Got Hit By The Train You Left On"), even British grunge rockers (as *The Surly Bitches* bashing out numbers from *Penis Free Planet)*! Will they stop at nothing? A medley of *Beach Boy's* surfer hits interpreted by *Ethel Merman* and *Kate Hepburn*? What could be more appropriate? Hilarious from git to go, and hands-down the best album cover of the year! Do we really want to encourage this type of thing? Hell, yes! Check out the band that inspired *Barney Clives* *(Consumer Report)* to rave: "Dos Fallopia...has a...certain...appeal." Irresistible lunatics.

How did you get your name? We discovered we were twin sisters of different cul-de-sacs. But our name keeps getting mangled in print. We've been called Dog Fallopia and Dos Fellatio, and we're hoping one day to be listed as Dog Fellatio.

MARK ETHEREDGE: AS DAWN (1990)

> **Twilight Productions**
> 725 Santa Susana Street
> Sunnyvale, CA 94086
> *AS DAWN*: CS $12.98...CD $17.98

Contemporary instrumental. As Dawn is a blending of acoustic and electronic textures in which keyboard and drum grooves complement the main voice, the grand piano. Several of these pieces sound like film themes (they may well be for future gay movies, television sitcoms or dramas!) Even the quieter, tender moments have an energy that rescue the album from New Age bloat. The percussion work of Christopher Miller adds energy to the pieces that are eloquent, simple, and yet powerful. The album will win you over with its ease and sweetness, and sophisticated grandeur that rivals *Yanni* at his best. A fresh, clean sound and a dazzling debut.

Why did you wish to categorize your instrumental album as gay music? I wrote these tunes during the process of coming out as a gay man. *As Dawn* is the beginning of freedom.

THE FABULOUS POP TARTS: GAGGING ON THE LOVELY EXTRAVAGANZA (1992)

Dance/club/house. Running through smooth dance grooves in *Erasure* and *Pet Shop Boys* territory without sounding so manically detached, the Pop Tarts connect in a strangely spiritual way in a medium (dance music!) typically *gagging on the lovely extravaganza* reserved for the shallowest of sentiment. Not nearly as alienating as the mass of house music being churned out today, this album speeds you along the freeway of love with no exit ramps. Guest luminaries include: *Dan Hartman, RuPaul* and *Dee-Lite's Lady Kier Kirby.* Trance-inducing tribal grooves and fractured vocal samples meld with Fenton Bailey's vocals for sexy, seductive effect. Two of the busiest men in show business, the Pop Tarts have

THE RETURN OF THE FABULOUS POP TARTS produced three hit television series (including *The Best of Manhattan Cable* for England's Channel 4), written a book (about *Michael Milken!*), masterminded the career of supermodel/singer *RuPaul,* and composed and recorded this 17-song CD—all in the past twelve months! Superachievers of the world! Someone has to stop these two before they take over the entertainment industry entire! But, if you've got to gag on anything, it might as well be these tarts.

> **World of Wonder**
> 80 Varick Street #7B
> New York, NY 10013
> *GAGGING ON THE LOVELY EXTRAVAGANZA*: CD $17

AMY FIX: AMY FIX (1993)

Folk. Amy Fix is a singer/songwriter, a violinist and a painter. She and guitarist *Sam Fenster* perform regularly around New England, and her eponymous release is her first recording. Hip, frank, queer, and set square in the folk/country groove, original songs like "Beautiful Dyke Ways," "Photograph of Jane," and "This Fruit" display fresh writing by this New York City artist. Her *Nanci Griffith* little girl voice captivates you immediately. The subject of incest is dealt with sensitively, passionately and terrifyingly in "Who Will Hold Me?" and only goes further to prove that Amy Fix is a writer of unmatched power on the cutting edge of the new musical frontier for women.

What is your creative process? I basically write whatever pops into my head, and the gayer the better. I never censor myself. My music departs from folk and draws on an eclectic assortment of musical styles.

How has music changed your life? Music saved my life. Music stirs people's deepest emotions and can be a very healing thing. So a lot of my songs are about my own healing from sexual abuse, and they offer hope and healing to the listener.

> **Amy Fix**
> PO Box 984
> New York, NY 10025-0984
> *AMY FIX*: CS $8.75

Why did you decide to forgo pursuing a mainstream career to do lesbian music? I *am* pursuing a mainstream career! I couldn't possibly censor my inspiration and still make good music. People of all walks of life respond warmly to my music because when I'm specific, it grabs people. I win them over because they can cling to the details even if the gender is different or the circumstances aren't the same. I want to be a big pop star who is out as a lesbian and out as an incest survivor from day one. When I first started writing songs, I assumed that only a few lesbian incest survivors would want to listen to them. But I kept getting such a great response from gay men, straight people, lesbian non-incest survivors...everybody! So, I'm just going along with what's happening, and if the rest of America responds the same way, then I suppose that's what mainstream success is.

THE FLIRTATIONS: THE FLIRTATIONS (1990)

A cappella. If there is one group that embodies the state of gay culture today, it's The Flirtations. The Flirtations gained national prominence in the late 80's as the only openly gay positive a cappella group. Oh, it helped that they had

tremendous voices and chose outstanding material. In a few short years, these media darlings became everybody's group of choice as ambassadors of homosexuality the world over. Their eponymous, fully digital premier contains some of their best-loved material: "To Know Him Is To Love Him," "Something Inside So Strong," "Everything Possible" and "Surfin' U.S.A." camped to perfection. A group like this only comes along once in a lifetime. Between the brilliant harmonies, general

silliness, and giddy repetoire, a splendid time is guaranteed for all.

THE FLIRTATIONS: LIVE--OUT ON THE ROAD

A cappella. The Flirtations have been thrilling audiences with their unique blend of musical artistry, politics and infectious humor since their first street corner appearance in Greenwich Village in the fall of 1988. Little could they have known that within five short years they would have appeared on *The Phil Donahue Show, Good Morning America, Nightwatch, MTV News* and *National Public Radio*; that they would have gathered rave reviews across the country; and that they would actually be making a living doing what they love most: being gay and singing about it. Stunning, exciting, moving, engrossing and hysterically funny, this album gives you a front row seat for the best gay act in America. Recorded in Vancouver in December 1992, *Out On*

The Road captures all the excitement of the Flirts' live performances. The album contains Flirts faves "Boy From New York City," "Johnny Angel," "Lesbian Love," "The Homecoming Queen's Got A Gun," and "Living In Wartime." There is a wonderful excitement to hearing the group live, and experiencing the audience interplay and reaction. An absolutely magnificent release!

What are The Flirtations all about? We perform a wide variety of musical styles, with an emphasis on songs that empower people to be who they are, songs that deliver some sort of political message, and songs that are just plain fun (primarily revamped doo-wop classics from the fifties). It's a fulfillment of our dreams to be lucky enough to perform as proud gay men in these times. We try to be entertainers first and musicians second. Our mission is political; we want to change the world, but we never want to bore people with the delivery of that message.

How do you hope your music will impact other people's lives? Music can inspire people to action, soothe those who are weary, and change minds and soften hatred in those who don't understand us. We are proud of many things, but we are most proud that people have played our songs at births, deaths, marriages, retirement parties, artificial inseminations, etc. We're proud that we can make a difference in someone's life.

What is gay and lesbian music, in your definition? All music is gay and lesbian music. Some of it just has the pronouns wrong.

Why did you choose a career path as gay musicians? To piss off our parents...No, actually our parents all love what we're doing. We decided to be out gay musicians because we just couldn't keep our wrists from flying in the air...No, that's not it either. I guess we just like being ourselves.

What is your vision of the future of gay music? One day we won't

> **The Flirtations**
> PO Box 421
> Prince Street Station
> New York, NY 10012-0008
> *THE FLIRTATIONS:* CS $12...CD $17
> *OUT ON THE ROAD*: CS $12...CD $17

have gay music—we'll just have music which lets us express our experiences without qualification.

Who are The Flirts top five favorite recording artists? Are you kidding? Do you think you could get us queens to agree on such a thing? We can probably agree that the following belong on the list, though: *Barbra & Bette, Sarah & Ella, Karen & Richard, Cris & Tret...*

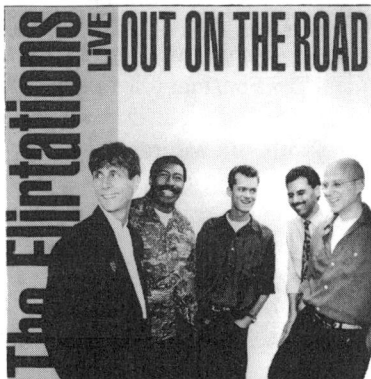

TED FOX: ONE OF US (1992)

Folk/pop. Uplifting, political, and stridently queer! The spirit is reborn in Ted Fox, and it is mighty! He is an out and proud gay man singing songs of defiance and positive self-affirmation. His debut features folkie melodies sung with self-assurance, and the social commitment and that *Peter, Paul and Mary* mined in the 60's hey-day of the folk form. The beautifully executed lyrics and the coffeehouse energy make this tape well worth a listen, and the sentiment comes through loud and queer. The richly layered harmonies and pop melodies hearken back to *The Mamas and The Papas*, and the songs are delivered with a distinct 60's pop radio feel. "Sink or Swim," an anthem for our struggle, is the real winner here. Handsome, long-haired, blond, and outspoken, no wonder Mr. Fox already has a devoted following of "Ted-Heads!"

Describe your music. My music is very personal. I try to write as if I were talking to a close friend. My musical style is closer to folk/rock than other categories, but there are influences from R&B to classical. My influences include my mom and dad, *The Beatles, Jonathon Edwards, Carole King* and on and on.

How has music impacted your life and how do would you like your music to touch other people's lives? Music saved my life. Music helped me to survive prison, high school, and being rejected by my family because of being gay. Music is a universal healer, and if one of my songs can help someone through a difficult time, or give someone strength, or let them know that they aren't alone in the way they feel, then I have been able to touch the Goddess. And from the letters I get, I *have* touched her. That makes me the luckiest man alive.

What prompted you to become an out gay artist? I have always been a performer and I've always been political, and this is how I'm making the world a better place...one voice being honest about loving myself against the odds. Plus, I believe that music about our lives has an uncanny ability to touch the lives of *all* people, especially anyone who's ever felt persecuted.

Edward Passino
1415 Steele Street #3
Denver, CO 80206
ONE OF US: CS $13

Where do you think gay music is headed? Gay music is just going to get bigger and bigger. Our voices cannot be silenced. And I honestly believe that soon, we are going to be all over the mainstream charts. Even if it gets slightly watered-down for those charts, as long as we can get our stories out there, then maybe our youth will stop feeling the need to kill themselves. Musical role models and heroes can change the world.

CINDY FREEDMAN: LIVE THE LIFE YOU DREAM (1990)

Acoustic folk/jazz. Freedman is a singer and musician who performs her delightful blend of Earth-Heart folk music at peace gatherings, festivals and retreats across Europe and the U.S. She also hosts a radio program in Houston, Texas, and guides people to the experience of the healing power of sound via singing, chanting, and percussion in her "Sound Harmony" workshops. She has impeccable good taste when it comes to choosing material, and she has selected the best. Without any pretense, she shows us how an album about peace, love, and Mother Earth can be effective and uplifting without sounding stodgy. She sings with calm reverence, and chooses material which conveys a reassuring feeling of universal peace, tranquility and union of spirit to create a compassionate, nurturing, moving listening experience that is seductively spiritual. Using music as the connector and common bond between people, "Dancers In The Light," "May The Light Of Love," and especially "OM/Jaya Mantra" are absolutely transcendental experiences. This album approaches the transcendent folk/jazz height *Van Morrison* achieved on *Astral Weeks*. Freedman's soulful flights practically stop time. The performance and spiritual lyrics on this release will make you swoon; the sound just shimmers. A disc of sheer loveliness and a blessed find!

Cindy Freedman
PO Box 66566
Houston, TX 77266
LIVE THE LIFE YOU DREAM: CS $12...CD $17

GENDERATION: GENDERATION (1993)

Dance/techno. John Dunton is a techno menace from Los Angeles, and the youngest entrant in the **GAY MUSIC GUIDE** at 21 years old. Influenced by *William Orbit, Mark Moore* and *Eon*, he determined to fill the gap he found in the existent club music. The result is a diverse, yet remarkably focused piece of work

John Dunton
PO Box 1478
Cypress, CA 90630
GENDERATION: CS $9

featuring hard-core dance music, tribal, and ambient selections, along with a few steamy vocal tracks. I admit that I never "got" Techno Music until I listened to Dutton's album. While searching for meaning in the compulsively rhythm-driven *seeming* chaos, I was struck by the Zen "duh!" Generation X and Techno Music intersect at precisely the point of the search-for-meaning-in-the-crumbs-of-what-remains of the world that's being left to the twenty-nothings. The *absence* of meaning is precisely the point! This goes way beyond alienation and rebellion into a psycho-frenzied hyper-weltschmerz. Dance into the daze. There is no tomorrow.

GOD IS MY CO-PILOT: STRAIGHT NOT (1993)

Punk. Jarring, disconbobulated, annoyingly noisy discord provides the setting for Sharon Topper's perky, mostly spoken, eerie readings of mindheadjabber penned by band-mate and husband, Craig Flannagin. Performance art? New Beat Poetics? Static jazz? The day you "get" God Is My Co-Pilot is the day you've reached the nirvana promised by the Zen masters once you've figured

GOD IS MY CO-PILOT

Straight Not

out the sound of one hand clapping. Recording for the homocore label *Outpunk* has called more attention to the gender terrorists aspect of the GodCo program. This large tribe of queers and straights, grrrls and boys together presents a protean, hard to pigeonhole vision of roles and their meanings, in and out of music (and in and out of the closet!) Musically abrasive and morally judgmental as the band is, their main strategy seems to be to beguile as much as to confront. Jump rope rhymes, hardcore thrash, and avant jazz are all equal parts of the

Outpunk
PO Box 170501
San Francisco, CA 94117
STRAIGHT NOT: CD $12

program. Since 1989, GodCo has recorded three albums, a 10" record and about ten 7" singles. Flannagin seems to want to mock sexual boundaries by writing girl love songs for his wife to sing. GodCo makes use of vocal distortion, experimental extremism, thrashingly manic energy, and fractured rock/jazz instrumental virtuosity to get their Queercore message across. **But, what is the message?** If you want a message, how about: so much noise in the world, so much sex, so many amazing things, and nothing happens that doesn't contradict itself in the happening, I think I will dance now.

SONYA HELLER: ALL OF THESE THINGS (1991)

Acoustic folk/jazz. A voice like *Phoebe Snow*, a rich ambient setting for her smoldering vocals and seductive guitar sound, and well-penned songs about the midnight places of the human soul, all add up to a winner on Sonya Heller's debut tape. A veteran of *The Bitter End* and *Speakeasy* in Greenwich Village, *WBAI Public Radio*, theatre productions, and *Woodstock '92*, she possesses a beautiful and unique lyrical style, and sings songs of love transformation and survival with an unmistakable feminine and peaceful determination. Folk, pop and jazz combine with Heller's unique contralto and dynamic guitar playing to produce an intimate and stirring listening experience. This tape is by far one of the most exciting discoveries of the year! Heller's spirit will send you right over the edge and into your bliss.

What has been your career experience? I hope I'm not disappointing anyone here by being the "token straight" musician who happens to have incredibly strong tribal/spiritual connections to the gay community in New York City and across the country. My audiences are gay, bisexual and straight. What we all have in common, at least in my "tribe," are sensitivity, and tolerance for free expression of spirit through our human-ness and well-meaning intentions while we all fumble through this thing called Life...clumsily perhaps, and sometimes when we're lucky, gracefully, with confidence and flair.

But you consider yourself an out musician? My music speaks for all of us who are truly living and feeling each step we take. Having been a musical artist most of my life, I know first-hand the isolation of being "different, odd, black sheepish, a witch and a dreamer." I didn't ask to be born with perfect pitch or haunted by melodies in

> **Sonya Heller**
> 103 East Second Street #2
> New York, NY 10009
> *ALL OF THESE THINGS*: CS $10.95

my dreams by the time I was three. I just am who I am. I'm an out musician who's serious about what she does because it's the only thing she can do. It is in this spirit that I connect to all "out" communities and support the struggles and triumphs of all people who don't quite fit the "American Dream" outlook on life.

What is your vision of the future of this genre? I hope that of all things, music can be instrumental in bringing harmony and awareness to all people, and can bridge the gap between cultures, races and expressions of sexuality.

LESLIE KILLE: STORM (1991)

Pop. "Driven By Madness," "The Other Side," and "I Miss You" are highlights on this keyboard-driven album completely arranged, produced and performed by Leslie Kille. There is a wonderful intimacy and purity about self-contained artists. (*Stevie Wonder, Prince* and *Paul McCartney* are artists who have put out hit albums written, produced and performed as solo outings). Kille's release is full of pretty, lush melodies to sway to. You can smell the sea salt air and hear the swoosh of the Florida surf that inspired many of these tracks. Kille has a full-time career as a psychologist, but somehow finds the time to write and produce marvelous music. Her voice sounds remarkably like *Emily Saliers* of *Indigo Girls,* and she uses it to sing sophisticated melodies and introspective, lesbian positive lyrics that make for an impressive first outing.

LESLIE KILLE: MOVING CLOSER (1992)

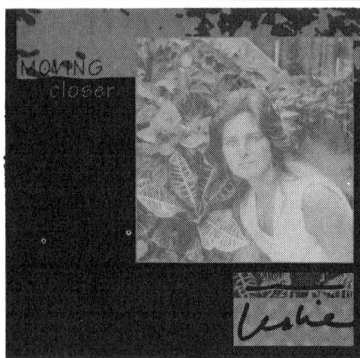

Pop/rock. A more sultry, rocking album than her debut puts Leslie Kille out front of a real live band, adding the mean, bluesy guitar work of *George Harris* and a tight rhythm section. The musical variety creates a listening experience that never lags. Kille fits somewhere between the melodic introspection of *Carole King* and the rock beat confidence of *Joan Armatrading.* She updates and brings new life to three of the best songs from her first album ("Hear Me

Leslie Kille
PO Box 10606
St. Petersburg, FL 33733
STORM: CS $8.50 (on sale!)
MOVING CLOSER: CS $11.50...CD $16.50

Now," "Storm," and "Driven By Madness"). This disc showcases the evolution of an artist from self-contained one-woman band to full production ensemble of musicians. *Moving Closer* t-shirts and tank tops also available (state size/style, each $9.50).

GRANT KING: WHERE TO NOW (1992)

GRANT KING
WHERE TO NOW

Folk/pop. Grant King's premier four-song tape captures surprisingly well the warmth and sensuousness of his live performances. King's easy, *James Taylor*-like charm oozes out of these tracks. Some of his more popular performance pieces are here, "To Hold and Be Held" and "Your Roses Came Today." His amazing rhythm guitar work drives "Loving Cup" in a manner reminiscent of *Lindsey Buckingham's* guitar work with *Fleetwood Mac*. He writes from the heart and never fails to win over audiences, and is and always has been an unflinching and proud gay singer/songwriter.

GRANT KING: ENTITLED TO BLOOM (1993)

Folk/pop. Grant King's latest release includes more heartfelt lyrics that are deeply personal, bringing you much closer to the artist. He uses the crystal clarion of his voice to communicate straight to your heart. Also featured on this tape is King's collaboration with *Rob Costin*, "James and Me," a sweet song sung from the perspective of an adoring child about the tall, strong, older brother he looks up to, that could well be the most innocently subversive song ever penned by a gay songwriter.

Describe your music and what you do. I'm a performing songwriter. My music has been called everything from New Folk to Art Songs. Much of it is in confessional style. My music has always been about trying to be honest about who I am and what I've experienced. For me, the personal *is* political. Although I've been writing songs since 1970, and came out in 1975, I've just begun actively pursuing recording and performing

Grant King

Entitled To Bloom

in the last two years, thanks in large part to the nourishing, rejuvenating and supportive environment created by *OutMusic*.

What has been the impact of music on your life? Music has saved my sanity on more than one occasion. It enriches my life beyond measure on a daily basis.

Why have you chosen the difficult road of being an out gay musician? Being gay is part of who I am, like having brown eyes. Since so much of my music is already so personal, it seems absurd to leave that part out. I've chosen to do music, period, and the gay part comes with the whole package. And I like to think that music *can* be my mainstream career. And I thank *Holly*

> **Grant King**
> c/o Open Secrets Musicworks
> PO Box 132
> Old Chelsea Station
> New York, NY 10113-0132
> *WHERE TO NOW*: CS $7
> *ENTITLED TO BLOOM*: CS $10

Near, Michael Callen (see listing), *Janis Ian, Romanovsky & Phillips* (see listing), *The Flirtations* (see listing), *k.d. lang* and all the others paving the way every day!

What is your vision of gay music? Recordings by gay artists in every library, school and community center around the planet. A gay *Lollapalooza* tour in the U.S. and abroad. A nationally distributed gay music show on both radio, TV and home video. An annual gay music festival like *OutMusic's*, only bigger and better funded. A gay national musical symposium that tours and encourages the musicians and composers among our lesbian and gay youth.

LISA KOCH: COLORBLIND BLUES (1991)

Pop. Lisa Koch (pronounced "Coke") is one the best things that's ever happened for gay and lesbian music. The impressive body of work by this influential artist includes *Dos Fallopia* (an outrageous comedy duo with comic *Peggy Platt*, see listing), *Venus Envy* (a funky feminist quartet, see listing*)*, *The Fabulous Dyketones*, and her solo work. She's an energetic and unstoppable talent, and I believe we really need to encourage this type of behavior. She has appeared regularly on Seattle stages and has co-written such memorable productions as *The Bouffants Go To The Beach, Dweeb Tales*, and *Rockin' Chain Gang Rebels.* Breezy jazz, smooth soul (check out the *Anita Baker*-like "All

> **Tongeinchic Productions**
> 1202 E. Pike, Suite 712
> Seattle, WA 98122
> *COLORBLIND BLUES*: CS $12...CD $15.99

Night Long"), doo-wop, plus her all-time classic "Beaver Cleaver Fever" (a tribute to late night television reruns with a decisively lesbo slant), all blend on this amusing and engaging disc. Her stirring AIDS anthem, "Light of A Memory" is one the top gay songs this year. Balancing comic songs, crafted ballads, and sublime jazz/pop, this non-stop entertaining disc put Lisa Koch squarely into the Top Ten, and in case *you're* colorblind, I'm giving this album the green light!

BEN & ELLIE KREADER: SINK OR SWIM b/w BLIZZARD— CASSINGLE (1993)

Synth/pop/soul. Surprise! The most promising debut of the year is this cassette single written and produced by substantial young talent Ben Kreader (pronounced "crater"). His sister, Ellie, takes vocal lead on the first track, "Sink or Swim." Ellie Kreader has a dream voice, a voice with the elasticity and how-dee-do of *K.T. Oslin*, able to convey every little quirk of emotion. The tracks are dark, rhythmic masterpieces that call to mind early work by *Eurythmics.* Ben Kreader's voice (he sings "Blizzard") is big, bluesy and R&B tinged. These two tracks are from an elaborate multimedia performance Ben presents that involves rear screen projection, hand-held lights, glowsticks, road flares, flashlights, and pinwheels that pulls 17 of his songs into a narrative story line. Ben began singing in college after placing an ad in the *Chicago Reader* for a woman who "smokes at least a pack a day." When nobody responded, he ended up discovering his own voice without the aid of Marlboros.

How would you describe your music? I make musical furniture. Songs you can sit down on or stack stuff on. I don't make anything fancy, just functional. If you use it every day or connect it directly to your day-to-day experiences, then I've done a good job. I try to use my sexuality as a viewpoint from which to better observe the world. I sing about pretty specific gay things sometimes, but I always try to say things in a way that anyone could relate to at some level. Everybody feels essentially the same things. They just like hearing somebody else say them once in a while. It's my little trick: I get people to identify with what I'm saying first, and then give them my context. It's made for some surprising fans.

Why have you chosen to do gay music? I don't think I've chosen anything.

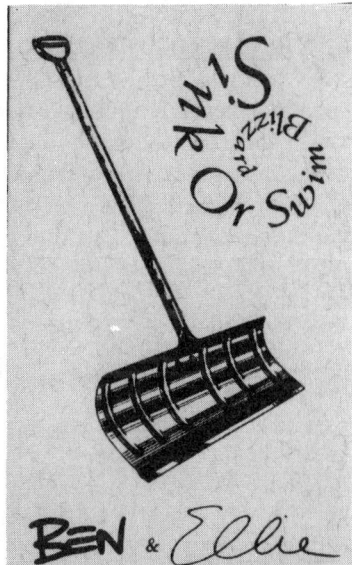

I'm just writing what I want to write. Being out isn't a badge I wear while I'm singing, it is simply who I am. I've never really wanted to be in anyone's face with my music. When I wrote a song that dealt with AIDS, it also could be seen as dealing with death in general. I like leaving things open

> **Ben Kreader**
> 1625 Chicago Avenue
> Evanston, IL 60201
> *SINK OR SWIM/BLIZZARD*: CS $7

while being very texturally specific. Being gay is just one of many things I am. Music is more important to me than who I sleep with. However, I fully appreciate the more political shoulders of people like *Jimmy Sommerville* who have allowed me to take this position. I'm not blind to my privilege.

What is your vision of gay music? I think gay music will participate in a bit of the 90's cultish trend to fragment the art communities into their respective cultural, regional and ethnic divisions. This will mean greater exposure for divisions that have not been traditionally status quo. Gay pop will become more visible and identified as such, but I have a feeling that this will just be the intermediate step towards a more diverse chorus of musical voices and not a permanent splinter in the music community. It can't be.

ROB KRIKORIAN: QUICKSAND IN THE HOURGLASS (1990)

Folk/pop. Rob Krikorian writes about time and love; how time passes and love heals. Krikorian's voice is perfectly suited to this mellow style of music popularized by *Dan Fogelberg* and others: contemporary folk for those with a taste for quiet music and with an interest in lyrics/imagery and a sense of humor. "Aren't We Born To Dance" is the most direct of the set, alluding to the *Stonewall* riots. The title songs deals with mortality in a particularly

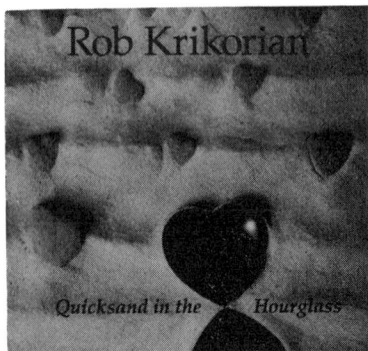

Rob Krikorian

Quicksand in the   Hourglass

moving manner, and "Send In $9.95" takes a jab at televangelists peddling Jesus. *Quicksand* is a lovely, polished work, a gentle disc on which Krikorian conveys a *Michael Franks'* style easiness and charm. The result is that you just like the guy and his tastefully produced, reflective, soft adult-contemporary sound.

What is your music all about? My music reflects my obsessions at any given time. The most recurring themes are love and relationships set against the passing of time. I am particularly fond of writing lyrics both serious and satirical.

What's it like being an out gay performer? Making an audience aware that I am gay makes me feel more able to communicate with them. For example, when I use the word "love," I want an audience to know what my concept includes. How do you hope your music will impact other people's lives? I would like my music to expand their concept of love; to make people think about the direction of their lives; to give people hope and energy to make the world better; to make them laugh; and to affirm life without denying its complexity, struggle or mystery.

How do you define gay music? I would use the broadest possible definition. Gay music is whatever music gay men and lesbians choose to create and is as diverse as our community. Is it gay music if it is created by someone who isn't the "outest" or the "proudest"? I'd prefer that, but who knows? The "outness" standard does seem difficult to apply to all places and eras.

LYNN LAVNER: BUTCH FATALE: LIVE IN CONCERT (1992)

Cabaret/comedy. Among the other achievements in her life, Lavner and her lover of 18 years are "co-parents of three daughters." They raised the girls—now in their 20's—together. Billed as "America's most politically-incorrect entertainer," Lavner is the winner of the 1991 *Christopher Street West* award for extraordinary creativity in lesbian and gay music and entertainment. She has performed at *NOW* events as well as the *International Mr. Leather Contest.*

Released in 1993, *Butch Fatale* is Lavner's fourth album, but the first recorded live-in-concert, and includes cabaret monologues and humor, as well as all-new songs. Her appearance (in black leather) is aimed at a playful parody of stereotypes. It's her ability to make you laugh one moment and cry the next that makes her impact unforgettable. Upbeat and thought-provoking, she bridges the gap between gay, lesbian and straight audiences, gets the audience cheering, and will warm your heart with her wonderfully human monologues. Standouts include "Gay 90's," "For The Children," and "I Think I've Been A Lesbian Too Long."

Describe you music and what you do. I perform a cabaret of original songs, humor, and serious monologues at the piano. The act is a polished one, in the style of Broadway and Tin Pan Alley, and appeals equally to lesbians and gay men.

Who would you name as your personal musical influences? I grew up loving the songs of the *Gershwins, Rodgers & Hart, Irving Berlin,* and the singing of *Judy Garland, Al Jolson, Marlene Dietrich* and *Elvis Presley.*

What is gay and lesbian music in your definition? It is the special talent of lesbians and gays to express ourselves in a unique and touching way. I've always believed that we're *different* from everybody else *except* for what we do in bed. I'd like to see my culture accessible to everyone. *Fiddler On The Roof* is a very specifically Jewish story and *Ain't Misbehavin'* is black music about the black experience, but both are accessible to and enjoyed by all audiences. The gay sensibility has that potential, too.

What is your vision of gay music? The beauty of music is that you never know its future, as long as writers are free to follow their hearts in creating it.

KRISTIN LEMS: OH MAMA! (1978)

Pop/rock/folk. Lems got her career off to a fine start from the first stirring pop song off her debut, "Not Yet." Over the breadth of her fourteen-year career, Lems has proved herself to be nothing less than a female *Billy Joel,* in the sense that she has an uncanny ability to tap into the zeitgeist and write songs that reflect the social subconscious of the times, deliver her message palatably

and melodically, and put across those pop melodies with expert production. Lems fans consider her a political bellwether. P.S., Lems is an avowed heterosexual who has written several songs that deal explicitly with society's problem with homosexuality ("How Nice"), and with AIDS ("Someone's Missing"). "The 50's Sound," from this tape, is not to miss: knocking nostalgia for the Dull Decade ("they're dancing to what oppressed us twenty years ago.") No strident feminist, she gets an important message over ever so gently with humor and compassion. Her song "Farmer" has been oft-covered ("Call me a farmer, not a farmer's wife."). "Mamary Glands" is (not surprisingly) a big hit with *Dr. Demento.* Kristin Lems deserves special praise for being an unmistakable original.

KRISTIN LEMS: IN THE OUT DOOR (1980)

Pop/rock/folk. The songs here are brave, funny, and endlessly quotable, with lyrics perceptive and literate. Lem's classic ballad about "heterosexual privilege," "How Nice," was recently featured in the *Marching For Freedom* video from NGLTF. The song has been covered by *Elliot Pilshaw* (see listing),

among others. Another classic, "Days of Theocracy" got the Religious Right's number in a Tin Pan Alley, *Tom Lehrer* style before *Reagan* even came to office! Lems, quite justifiably, has proudly boasted that she can write a song on any topic. Her gift is her famous versatility, and ability to match musical styles ranging from calypso, honky-tonk, ballad and traditional folk to the spirit of the message of the verse.

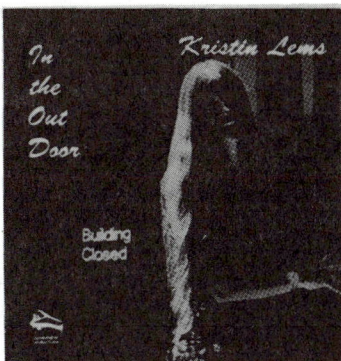

In the Out Door

Kristin Lems

Building Closed

KRISTIN LEMS: WE WILL NEVER GIVE UP (1982)

Pop/rock/folk. Recorded at an ERA rally in D.C. the day the ERA deadline expired, her live tape captures the excitement of a folkie protest rally and gives

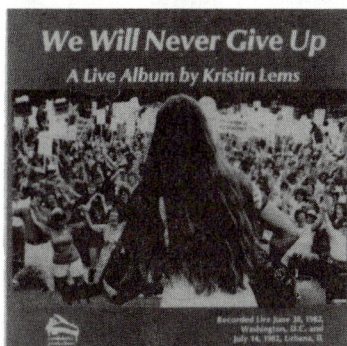

We Will Never Give Up
A Live Album by Kristin Lems

you the same chills you got hearing *Bob Dylan* sing "The Times They Are A-Changing." Protest music, for God's sake, that is relevant and rousing! Now, tell me music can't save the world. You cannot, after listening to Ms. Lems. This release features well-known feminist activist classics "I'm Gonna Be An Engineer," the moving title song, "My Mom's A Feminist," and "Ballad of the ERA." The predominant theme is two-fold: celebration of herself and of life in general, and the word of the women's movement. The live energy is a real battery starter for burned out organizers and newcomers to social justice issues.

KRISTIN LEMS: UPBEAT (1992)

Pop/rock/folk A male quartet from *The Fest City Singers* (a gay & lesbian chorus from Milwaukee, Wisconsin) sings on three songs on Lem's latest album which includes the moving "Someone's Missing," a song commemorating artists lost to AIDS. Feminist themes predominate, especially on "You Can't Beat A Woman" and "Mommy Track." But her songs of hope, whimsy, faith and pluck strike the strongest chords: "Life Has Other Plans," "Make The Best Of Your Life," "Each Child Is A Star," and "I Wish You A World." This is a terrific introduction to a wonderful artist who deserves our attention.

Describe what you do as an artist. I sing and play piano and guitar in many venues, celebrations and protests of all kinds, schools, coffeehouses and bars, occasional solo concerts, and conferences. Audiences are small but fervent, interactive, respectful and loyal, but I repeat, small.

Who are some of your personal artistic influences? *Ralph Nader, Catherine MacKinnon, Barbara Mikulski, Jacques Cousteau,* also *Harry Belafonte, Cat Stevens, Phil Collins, Supertramp, Pete Seeger, Holly Near...*I try to draw on many musical idioms in writing and in choosing repetoire.

How do you think music impacts people's lives? Music allows us all a space to feel and explore our thoughts. It's so powerful for that reason. And singing together (singalongs, etc.) is empowering and moving, a kind of spiritual experience.

Any thoughts about gay and lesbian music? I think it could doom its artists, the way "Women's Music" has. But, I

> **Carolsdatter Productions**
> 221-C Dodge
> Evanston, IL 60202
> *OH, MAMA*: CS $11.50
> *IN THE OUT DOOR*: CS $11.50
> *WE WILL NEVER GIVE UP*: CS $11.50
> *UPBEAT*: CS $11.50...CD $15.50

think there should be a gay strand in all types of music that identifies itself as such without getting cut off from "straight" music. Music is one field where difference is welcome already; the problem is the sexism, racism and homophobia in the radio stations, distributors, booking agents etc., not with the performers or audiences.

LIBANA: A CIRCLE IS CAST (1986)

Contemporary folk, rounds, chants. Libana is New England's premier World Music ensemble, and has been entertaining audiences for thirteen years. Based in Boston, Libana's eight women present a scintillating performance that features exquisite Balkan harmonies, frenzied Egyptian drumming, graceful Hawaiian melodies, and many more diverse cultural expressions united to evoke a spirit of determination and joy. Their 1986 release is a wonderful

collection to sing along with, take to ritual/spiritual groups, and is also used extensively by music educators. An extremely accessible work, it has been a best-seller since its release. The rounds and chants will lull you into a seductive trance the way an *Enya* recording does. This all-woman group of singers and musicians draws on Native American, African, Anglo, Israeli, European, Renaissance and contemporary folk sources to produce a truly unique collection of pieces. Ancient melodies speak with remarkable clarity; contemporary tunes articulate timeless sentiment. All of this expresses the spiritedness of people's lives worldwide, inspiring the listener with wonder in the commonality of the global community. The overall experience is hypnotic; the music connects

> **Ladyslipper, Inc.**
> PO Box 3124
> Durham, NC 27715-3124
> 1-800-634-6044
>
> *A CIRCLE IS CAST*: CS $12.73...CD $18.73...Songbook $11.73

you to the elemental world spirit and releases deep feelings of peace and enchantment. An incredibly special experience from a one-of-a-kind performance unit, it is no wonder this group has sold 50,000 albums and tours world-wide year round.

LAURA LOVE: Z THERAPY (1990)

Alternative folk/rock/funk. Over the past several years, Love has become quite acclaimed in the Northwest music scene as an unparalleled vocalist, songwriter and bassist. Her style is a synthesis of inner-city street funk n' soul and folkish sensibility. Having settled in Seattle, the mecca of all-things-garage, she was founding member of the grunge/blues outfit, *Boom Boom G.I.,* alternatively hailed as the best rock band in the city and reviled as the worst. Love went on to co-found *Venus Envy* (see listing) before embarking on a solo career. *Z Therapy* is her debut disc. From the rockabilly groove of "I'm Gonna Lay By My Friend Gi" to the Indian raga of "Leave My Head Alone," this album, recorded in Austin, Texas, reflects the earthiness of a city whose spiritual leader is *Willie Nelson.* A milestone in the evolution of a terrific artist, this disc presents some remarkable moments. "Swing Low, Sweet Chariot" is a show-stopper, and "Things I've Heard People Think" presents an intellecually sobering side to the AIDS crisis. Love enthusiastically throws everything into the stew with talent bursting at the seams, but what escapes her is a unified focus point for this work. That's a minor point when you consider that you are bombarded with musical brilliance that is consistently engaging throughout the duration of this album. With a finely developed social conscience and the soul of a true "people's poet," Laura Love carves a niche for herself in gay pop that only she could ever fill. She deals with issues like Silence, radiation poisoning of workers and corporate cover-up, and healing from personal emotional pain in her most unique gospel church / alternative voice that defies comparison.

LAURA LOVE: PANGAEA (1992)

Alternative folk/rock/funk. Laura Love has one of the most unique voices in New Women's Music; to hear her once is an unforgettable experience. Love's lyrics speak of hard choices and the struggle to overcome sorrow, buoyed by optimism. *Pangaea,* a more focused album than her 1990 release, showcases the extraordinary band Love assembled in Seattle, Washington in 1992. With this release, Love really comes into her own, finding her power and the best settings for her sociopolitical songs. She can be shatteringly vulnerable, but the thrust of this album is funk propelled by Love's poppin' bass. Highlights include the yodelled chorus of "Anyway," the reggae-inspired "Whenever Time Will Come," and "All Our Lives." Love is so far above and beyond anyone else that comparisons don't do her justice. This is a must-to-hear for her distinctive vocal and bass style, and songs that are bittersweet, undeniably compelling, politically progressive anthems of hope and social justice.

How do you describe your music? I often call my music Afro-Celtic, as it encompasses Afro-pop, Celtic, Appalachian, funk and folk. Some of my influences are *The Jackson Five, Karen Carpenter, The Drifters, Joni Mitchell, Steely Dan, Laura Nyro, Ferron* and *Shawn Colvin.* I have purposely chosen to do music that reflects my personal experience, which includes my gaiety.

What has been the impact of music on your life? Music got me through a really crappy childhood. I'm really glad I had a transistor radio when I was living through what otherwise was a really bad time. I hope my music reflects triumph over tragedy and is also easy on the ears.

What is gay and lesbian music in your definition? Anything that we want to listen to is gay and lesbian music. In my opinion, all music that can be enjoyed or listened to by anyone who is gay or lesbian is gay/lesbian music. This would include, but not be restricted to everything from *Madonna* to *Nirvana.*

Laura Love
PO Box 30853
Seattle, WA 98103
Z THERAPY: CS $12.50...CD $17.50
PANGAEA: CS $12.50...CD $17.50

What is your vision of gay music's future? Just that the boundaries will become much broader and many performers/artists/writers who are now confined to small sections of obscure bookstores will become mainstream the way *k.d. lang* and *Melissa Etheredge* have.

TOM McCORMACK: RUNNING WITH LIGHT (1991)

Pop/vocal. McCormack's debut showcases his more subdued, spiritual side, and contains some devastating songwriting, most notably on "Everything," which *Billboard* called "a warm and affecting ballad of earnest delivery complemented by a stark, piano-dominated arrangement." Sensual/sexy and spiritually attuned, this is an album conducive to spiritual journeying. The lyrics on *Running With Light* show a deep questioning and an awareness of how approaching God may involve not only faith, but a simultaneous exploration of both the soul and the psyche. The album finds power in its simplicity; the intimate setting of piano, voice and guitar elicits a personal response, inviting each listener to become part of the experience rather than remain a passive observer. *Running With Light* speaks with the language of the heart to a contemporary audience that yearns to mine more deeply the power of each person's passionate journey. McCormack represents the best our community has to offer. His outstanding voice, superb writing and production skills, and inspiring artistry embody the future of gay music. It's hard to decide which side of McCormack I love more: this more subdued, intimate side or his all-out rock follow-up. Instantly listener-friendly in the manner of *Elton John*, this is a stunning debut.

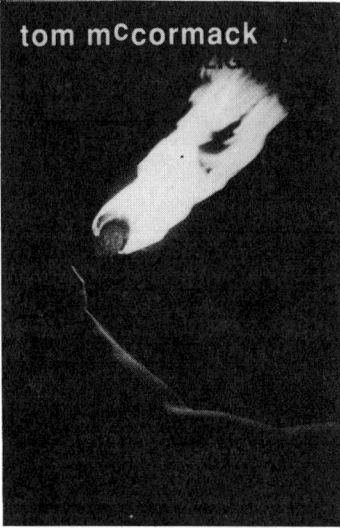

TOM McCORMACK: ROSE COLORED GLASSES (1993)

Rock/pop. Tom McCormack has one of the strongest, most appealing voices in gay pop music. His vocals are truly magnificent, and the production on this CD shines. He uses a rock sound that is an intentional throwback to the seventies sound; at times recalling *Billy Joel, Elton John* and *Crosby, Stills, Nash and Young.* The themes of his songs are more universal in that he does not speak directly to the gay experience as much as to the universal experiences of everyone who is questing. This kick-ass set of astonishing songs includes "I Am Alive," "Here I Am," and current crowd-pleaser, "Falling Down Kind Of Love," as he journeys still deeper on his second album into the gray areas of life with stories of money, desire and identity. Many of his songs are epiphanies, with moments of recognition when choices are offered and truth is either pursued or denied. Although he says he is looking at the world through rose colored glasses, McCormack's vision is startlingly clear. Here is someone who not only sees but asks to be seen. If the strength of this work is any indication, he indeed will be seen as a writer with something to say, as a singer with the voice to say it, and as an artist with his own unique way of looking at the world. Far and away the best rock album of the year!

What has been the impact of music on your life? Music was always my refuge. It helped me find out what was going on within me. Often music is a means for spiritual discovery and expansion. Music can give a common expression for people who may not be able to articulate what they feel within.

TOM McCORMACK

ROSE COLORED glasses

What is gay and lesbian music in your definition? Music created by gay and lesbian songwriters/composers that speaks to gay experience. I don't think it is necessarily explicitly stated that it's gay (same sex love song) nor is it necessarily unable to speak to non-gay experience.

As a talented person who has the choice of pursuing a mainstream career, why have you chosen to do gay music? Because I see my music as part of my own pursuit of "truthful experience." Besides, I wish there were more out performers when I was growing up.

What do you think the future holds for gay music? That gay music as such will not be set aside or made separate. It should not be a big deal that someone is gay or lesbian and a professional musician/songwriter.

Spotted Dog
PO Box 40-0041
Brooklyn , NY 11240-0041
RUNNING WITH LIGHT: CS $11.98
ROSE COLORED GLASSES: CS $11.98...CD $15.98

RUS McCOY: THE ACE SESSIONS (1991)

Alternative rock/ pop. McCoy is an out gay performer born to write and sing affecting alternative rock. The arrangements soar thanks to Ace, his producer/collaborator, and set him squarely in *Simple Minds/New Order/Depeche Mode* territory. "Never Tell A Soul" is a synth-pop standout that deals with alienation, self-induced silence and internalized homophobia. With guitar work that demands striking comparison to *U2's Edge*, songs like "Happy Birthday, Baby Butch" grab your ears immediately. From ambitious *Springsteen*-like suites to a sound reminiscent of early L.A. New Wave, McCoy hits the mark every time. He is an artist to watch! Dissonant, moody, synth-heavy dance music mixes with strong songs in the synth-rich dance/pop vein. The tracks are radio-ready, with sweeping cinematic soundscape settings for these socially conscious gems. Of special note: McCoy alone at the piano singing "I'm The Man" for the finale...heaven! This is one of the best-sounding, most well-conceived albums of late, from an artist whose ultimate goal is to be an openly gay rock artist who achieves regular airplay on mainstream radio.

Describe your music. I consider my music "Alternative Rock," mainly because under that title I am free to experiment in all areas like R&B, folk, country, grunge, etc. within a rock context. I tend to be more sociopolitical in my songs, as I tell stories about the world in which we live as gay and lesbian individuals. **What has been the impact of music on your life?** To me, music can bring down the walls of Jericho. People who seem unreachable through verbal debate can hear a song lyric that can stick to their consciousness and change them from within. Music has gotten me through tough times, like when I was coming to terms with my sexuality. Though none of the artists on the radio were (openly) gay, it was good to hear someone singing about loneliness and that it is all right to be different. Because I am openly gay, I hope to reach many people, especially gay teenagers, so they can know they're not alone. I want to deal frankly with hard feelings and say "Yes, it's tough, but be proud and strong, you're going to make it!"

What is your definition of gay and lesbian music? I think that to define it is to limit its possibilities. *Elton John, Melissa Etheredge* and *k.d. lang* are out, but their music rarely, if ever, reflects their homosexual orientation. That's their right, and what they do is still gay music because they are. Some gay artists have the word "gay" or "queer" in every song and are really in your face about their gayness. Others, like me, fall somewhere in between.

Why have you chosen to do gay music? Is this a wise career choice? The gay market is virtually untapped by major record labels. We tend to have more disposable income and buy more records. I'd like to tap into that market in a major way. Other artists like *Village People* and *Boy George* have cracked the door open and I, with the help of others, want to bust the door down. Record companies will respond when they see major money can be made. I hope my blend of melodic rock with lyrics that are out (but subtle enough to seduce the non-gay ear) will do the trick.

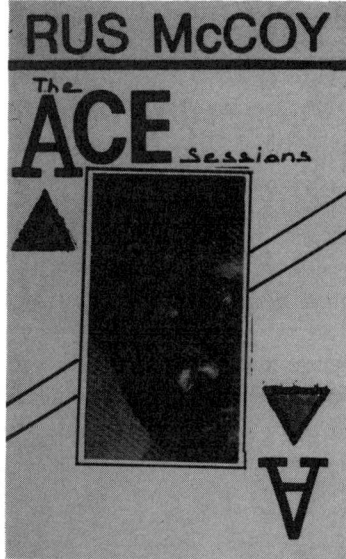

Rus McCoy
PO Box 131
Culver City, CA 90232-0131
THE ACE SESSIONS: CS $12

How would you like to see gay music develop? I would like to see gay music become mainstream, just another ingredient thrown into the mix of Top Forty and beyond. All these years we've listened to straight love songs and turned the "she's" into "he's" (and vice versa) so we could personalize the songs to fit our lives. It won't hurt the non-gay audience to do the same if a gay love song enters the charts. It's important that non-gay listeners are exposed to queer music, because the one revelation that will become very clear is the fact that we laugh, love and cry the same. We have many more similarities than differences.

BILL McKINLEY: EVERYTHING POSSIBLE (1992)

Pop/vocal. It is the rare performer who emerges and is granted instant and universal legendary status, but the sheer power of Bill McKinley's musical gifts have propelled him into mythic stature in a few short years. He is a showman and artist who possesses that winning combination of show biz savvy and utter naturalness that is the unmistakable mark of The Genuine Article. His debut release documents nothing less than the birth of a legend. With his incredible tenor instrument, McKinley interprets some exceptional material including: "And So It Goes" *(Billy Joel)*, "Love Don't Need A Reason" *(Callen/Malamut/Allen)*, "Children Will Listen" *(Stephen Sondheim)*, "Everything Possible" *(Fred Small, see listing)*, and "Disneyland" (from the Broadway musical *Smile*). An openly gay performer on the cabaret circuit, McKinley's talent is so electrifying that he deserves his own 76-piece orchestra on call 24-hours a day. There is a purity to McKinley's vocal styling that is contemporary and American standard at the same time. Remember *La Streisand*'s vocal rendering of "Happy Days Are Here Again" on *her* debut? It made her a star (okay...a *bigger* star) and assured her a ticket to superstardom. McKinley has likewise found new meaning in "This Land Is Your Land," translated in such a way as to make it his for all time. He coddles his inner child in a way that is healing and cleansing to the point of annoyance, but that is the brilliance of this concept album: it is dedicated to the inner child in each of us. "Danny Boy" is the album's moving tribute to everyone we've lost. Fresh, subtle and a showcase for astonishing technique, *Everything Possible* is a beautiful gift to the community, and is so stunningly brilliant, it leaves you gasping. A command performance, this is not just an album, it's an arrival.

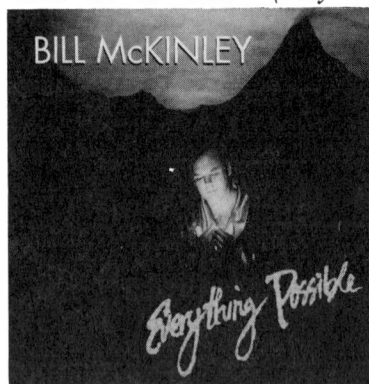

What is your music all about? More than gay music, I consider my music to be about the diversity in me, and in each of us. That certainly includes music about being gay, and I sing the pronouns that are appropriate for me, but since I consider myself to be much more than my sexual orientation, my music reflects that belief.

Who are your personal artistic influences? *Bette Midler, Walt Disney, Whoopi Goldberg, Barbra Streisand, Michael Callen, The Flirtations.*

What has been the impact of music on your life and how would you like your music to make a difference in other people's lives? Music is the way I have given voice to my soul. I think the musical tastes of our community are as diverse as anyone else's. However, I do think we're starved for music and entertainment that reflects us, and that most of us are so unaccustomed to being affirmed for who we are, that our first experience with openly gay and lesbian music is often disconcerting. I hope my music will help people fill out their own lives more, and help them be more of who they really are.

> **Everything Possible**
> PO Box 1483
> Indianapolis, IN 46206-1483
> *EVERYTHING POSSIBLE*: CS $14...CD $19

WILL McMILLAN: WILL SINGS SONDHEIM (1992)

Vocal/cabaret. This is a remarkable album of intelligent and senstive interpretations of Sondheim classics that span the songwriter's career, and even includes "More," written for the *Dick Tracy* soundtrack. The tribute is actually a soundtrack itself, taken from McMillan's one-man show in which he begins as a tuxedoed man and gradually transforms himself into a woman and then back into a man. The songs are performed with the reverential emotion and loving restraint of an adoring fan. There are also some playful (re)arrangements that shine new light on these classic theatre gems. Entertaining, and a welcome relief from those over-the-top ultra-theatrical Sondheim tributes of late, this is a collection that has been praised by the master himself!

Will Sings Sondheim

> **Will McMillan**
> 8 Westwood Road
> Somerville, MA 02143-1518
> *WILL SINGS SONDHEIM*: CS $10

DAN MARTIN: HOMO LOVE SONG (1990)

Pop/vocal. Dan Martin and Michael Biello are the fathers of the newly born gay music scene and are responsible for many new artists coming to light in our community. Martin has written scores for films and videos including *Clones In Love*, winner of *The San Francisco Gay & Lesbian Film Festival*'s top prize for Best Short. His score for *Lauren Malkasian's* video *The Last Run* is currently being aired on *PBS*, and his score for *Jim Hubbard's The Dance* (which chronicles Martin and life-partner Michael Biello's relationship) has screened at *The Berlin Film Festival, MOMA*, and at festivals around the world. He has also written instrumental music for *Hazelden Publishing's SOUND RECOVERY* series of subliminal healing cassettes, and for *EROSPIRIT's* sexual environments series. Martin is the founder of *OutMusic*, the organization of lesbian and gay composers, lyricists and musicians, which produces the only annual festival of gay and lesbian music. He has brought to the stage numerous queer music-theatre pieces with Biello, a performing visual artist and Martin's lyricist. On their debut release, the material is riveting, so you don't mind the spare piano/vocal production, though this artist deserves the full treatment. Martin's delivery runs the gamut from downright bratty (when called for) to heartbreakingly tender. This release introduced two gay standards: "Forgive Me," and the much-covered "Hold Me In Your Arms." Compassionate, raunchy, romantic and beautiful, the songwriting talents of Martin and Biello seem unending. This tape showcases a tremendous depth and range of emotion. Plus: butt shots on the album cover!

DAN MARTIN & MICHAEL BIELLO: HUMAN BEING (1992)

Pop/rock. Passionate performers of sensitive and perceptive material, Dan Martin and life partner/lyricist Michael Biello have become two of the most covered and cherished songwriters in our community. From anthems like "You Do Not Know Me" and "Lay Your Burden Down" to the butt-shaking beat of "Drag Dance" and the mechanical dance rhythms of "Strange

Now," *Human Being* delivers consistent entertainment pleasure. The spiritually uplifting pieces are emotionally ardent songs that resonate in the heart and soul. This is a perfect album of beautiful simplicity of arrangement, honestly observed sentiment, tasteful production, and stirring vocal styling. The growth in writing and (especially) production from their debut is startling. There is no waste on this album of mini-masterpieces. A *must* for every collection of indispensible gay and lesbian albums.

What do you like best about being an out gay performer? I love being an out gay performer because I can express my true self in my work, and I can share my music with gay audiences that specifically understand what I'm saying.

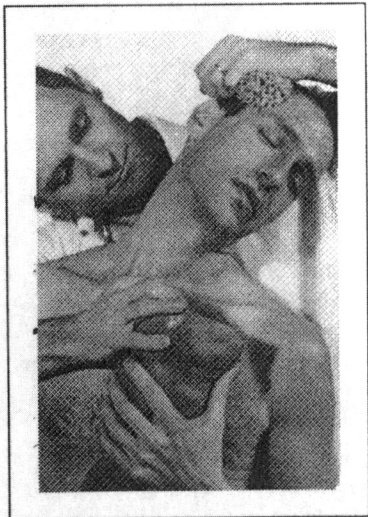

HŪ@MĂN@BĒ@ĪNG

DAN MARTIN
MICHAEL BIELLO

What has been the impact of music on your life? Music has been a great healing force in my life, as well as an agent of self-discovery. I am drawn to creating music that deeply moves people, that awakens some deep unspoken spirit within others (and myself). I would like people to listen to my music and feel both supported and challenged at the same time: supported and affirmed in the honesty of the self-expression, and challenged to tap into deep, expansive feelings.

What is your working definition of gay music? Gay and lesbian music is widely defined; any music created by self-identified lesbians or gays is gay music. The kind of gay and lesbian music I like best is the kind that has gay-specific lyrics; that simply and unapologetically uses same-sex pronouns. I also think gay music in 1994 often brings into play an intelligence shaped by living with AIDS, discrimination, and at its most evolved, an attempt to express healing that transcends this intelligence.

Why have you chosen a career as a gay artist rather than a more mainstream path? I'm an out gay musician because I have to be. I started writing songs in the mid-70's that simply and honestly expressed my coming out stories. I continued in this for ten years until I took a short detour in the hope of "fitting in" to what was marketable within the music industry. I spent three painful years suppressing myself and looking for approval until my inner voice couldn't take it anymore and started screaming. I found my way back to my own truth, I founded *OutMusic* to surround myself with others like me, and here I am!

What is your vision for the future of gay music? My vision for gay music is already manifesting, with more and more artists coming forth and making recordings. I'd like to see gay music develop the way gay publishing has (lots of independent record companies, divisions of major labels dedicated to gay and lesbian artists, retail stores with large sections of gay music, and a category at the Grammy's for gay music). I see more and more gay artists able to support themselves well through their music.

> **Dan Martin**
> PO Box 1575
> Canal Street Station
> New York, NY 10013
> *HOMO LOVE SONG*: CS $10
> *HUMAN BEING*: CS $12

GUSTAVO MOTTA: SONGS 1963-1993 (1993)

Piano/vocal. This abundant tribute to Gustavo Motta, who died in 1993, is a collection of thirty years worth of intelligent songwriting in traditions that borrow from cabaret, theatre, pop/rock and world influences. Motta's songs have been performed in concerts and cabarets in New York, San Francisco and Philadelphia during years when he was also staging productions for the *Houston Grand Opera*, the *Washington Opera*, and *Cincinnati Conservatory of Music* and at the *Metropolitan Opera*. Only after testing positive for HIV in 1987, did he devote himself full-time to recording and performing his music in solo concerts and AIDS benefits, and began an effort to ensure that his songs would be preserved and performed. The four cassettes feature dozens of dramatic songs by a superb craftsman who was at work on this collection right up to the end, and whose last spoken word was "Celebrate!" And there is much to celebrate here. At his best (and these songs are uniformly excellent), Motta ranks with *Stephen*

> **Barbara Lutz**
> Motta Music
> PO Box 1245 Cathedral Station
> New York, NY 10025
> *SONGS 1963-1993*: All four CS plus lyric book $45
> ...or each CS $12 (specify Tape 1, 2, 3, or 4)...Lyric book alone $7

Sondheim as a songwriter born to the craft. The four tapes contain treasures that anyone who performs cabaret or is a fan of the theatrical song should surely investigate. Readings by male and female voices lend nuance to the song interpretations, and they all feature Motta himself on piano. Motta's thirty year output reveals a super tunesmith whose songs deserves good homes. Singer/performers take note.

MUSICA FEMINA: RETURNING THE MUSE TO MUSIC (1989)

Flute/guitar duo. Since 1983, the duo has brought to concert stages across the country little-known music by forgotten women composers in a format that offers both music and music history not currently available from other artists today. This disc recreates their concert format by introducing dynamic women composers from the early 1600's (some of the earliest known musical works by women) to the present day. Musica Femina has restored and revived the reputations of classical women composers hidden by history's prejudices, and for that they deserve our praise. They want to make it clear that women were present in music history, and for the most part have been excluded from the standard texts. I learned about women like *Elizabeth de la Guerre*, who lived at the court of *Louis XIV*, and was a famous musician and composer in her day, who have been literally written out of music history; as well as more obscure women like *Fanny Mendelssohn, Mendelssohn's* sister, whose music was often appropriated by her brother and published under his name. Great music and fascinating history.

MUSICA FEMINA: HEARTSTREAMS (1993)

Flute/guitar duo. In their latest release the duo presents their own compositions and uncanny ability to vary the tempos, styles and sounds they get from their instruments. The musical mix includes tango, gypsy Flamenco, Scottish, and Renaissance styles from two contemporary classical composers who should be celebrated in our community. A terrific instrumental album of all-original acoustic chamber music.

What has been the impact of music on your lives? In the 70's, Women's Music was the glue that held the newly emerging women's culture together. It was very exciting and affirming to hear women sing about our real lives. Today, we offer our audiences a chance to know us as lesbians, as well as musicians. We find that our honesty and candor is accepted once the musical connection has been made.

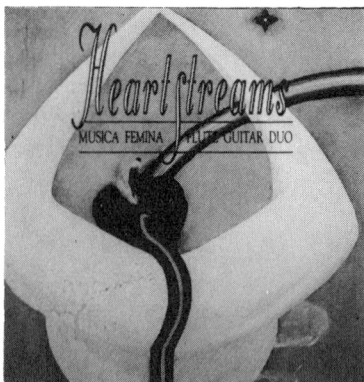

And how do you define gay/lesbian music? Any music performed by lesbian and gay people who are clearly comfortable being who they are—in other words, "out artists."

Why have you chosen to label yourselves "out artists?" Because we think it's important for everyone to know who we are, and what wonderful contributions lesbians and gays make to our mainstream culture. In this era of backlash, we must be out as often as we can.

Who are some of your influences? We have been influenced by *Kay Gardner, Sharon Isbin, Sweet Honey In The Rock, Alix Dobkin* (see listing), *Jamie Anderson,* and many others.

What is your vision of the future of gay music? In classical music, the more of us who come out, the easier it will be for the younger people who follow us. And the more comfortable the public becomes with gay/lesbian people through us being out,

> **Musica Femina**
> PO Box 15121
> Portland, OR 97215
> *RETURNING THE MUSE TO MUSIC*: CS $11.50...CD $16.50
> *HEARTSTREAMS*: CS $11.50...CD $16.50

the sooner we will find acceptance of civil rights for our community.

JOHN ORLANDO: DRUM SONGS (1993)

Percussion/instrumental/world beat. A former and original member of the *San Francisco Gay Marching Band* as well as *Denver's Mile High Freedom Band,* Orlando is regarded as a musical ambassador of the gay community. One evening in the late 70's, as the only drummer, he led the candlelight march of thousands of mourners in San Francisco for the (then) recently slain *Harvey Milk.* He has performed in swing bands, Dixieland bands, even a gay New Wave punk band, the techniques and styles of which have culminated in his current, highly personal style evident on this release. Soothing and invigorating at the same time, it's amazing that an all-percussion record could be this interestingly conceived and so much fun to listen to. It is a totally new and different listening experience that will leave you positively energized. Orlando uses over twenty-one percussion instruments plus live crickets, birds and frogs to hypnotic effect. The timbre of unsynthesized drums native to many lands create unexpected melodies. Maybe it's because I live near the New York City's Hare Krishna headquarters and I've come to love the daily afternoon tambourine jams, but John Orlando demonstrates that percussion instruments can be combined to create beautifully exotic music. (Or maybe it's because my lover dances around the apartment naked when I play the CD!) This music will make you move, and connect you to the primitive urges inside that want to express the life spirit through dance and movement. Instruments include congas, a darabucca, a kalimba, gourds, sacred chimes, a djembe, and more.

How do you describe your music? My music is all-percussion without drum machines. I also blend in some animal sounds. I create melodies with just drums.

How did this album come about? I wanted to create songs that used real (as opposed to synthesized) percussion instruments exclusively. Through my travels in the Southwest, I found Native American rattles and drums, and over time developed a collection of drums indigenous to many lands. Over the years, I arranged these percussion instruments and sounds of nature into exotic drum songs. The natural timbre of the drums gave each song a soothing spirit of the earth. Crickets from California forests and meadow birds from Colorado's lush marshes added nature's own color. More traditional percussion instruments and my years of experience with so many styles of music supported these songs with fusion and structure. Sound effects such as reverb and echo were used sparingly to preserve the natural timbre of the instruments. I offer my songs to the earth from which they rumble. I accept the challenge of reclaiming the spirit of natural drums for our world confused with the toxins of synthetic music.

How do you create songs from what are essentially rhythm instruments? The challenge was to make drums the main instrument without being repetitive. I always believed that drums in and of themselves could be interesting and entertaining. So, *Drum Songs* was an experiment for me. They say that drumming styles from African and Native American ceremonies can put you in a trance state. Sometimes my hands are channeled to beat rhythms which surprise even me!

Does being such a purist have anything to do with your move to Colorado? Sure. I am now living amongst the ancient red rock formations of the Rocky Mountain foothills. I accept these songs from the spirit of drumming with whom I have played throughout my life.

ANDREW PARALIC: THREE TUNES (1993)

Jazz. Composer/pianist Andrew Paralic has produced a sparkling three-song tape. His facility for jazz composition and his ensemble's supple execution of these jazz gems will leave you wanting more. Paralic is a graduate of *Baruch College*, and has attended the *Berklee College of Music* and the *Jazz Mobile*. The pieces on this release were written about reflections of his own gayness with titles like "Too Little, Too Late" (about AIDS funding), "Out Tune," and "Finally" (about the total acceptance of his lifestyle by his family). *Three Tunes* features amazingly sophisticated jazz from a brilliant young man with a bright future in the genre.

Who are some of your personal artistic influences? *Bill Evans, Thelonius Monk, Erik Satie, Lester Young...Talking Heads, The Smiths*!

Why do you label your jazz instrumental music "gay music?" Visibility has always been a goal and inspiration for me as a gay man. I'd like to be able to produce the best music I possibly can without anyone caring about my sexuality. Hopefully, someday gay musicians will be judged solely on their music.

> **Andrew Paralic**
> PO Box 20231
> New York, NY 10011
> *THREE TUNES*: CS $5

DAVID PAUL: NOEL COSMIQUE (1993)

New age/holiday. Canadian keyboardist David Paul has created a hip, enchanting delight for the holidays that has displaced my well-worn *Manheim Steamroller* discs. Intricate and surprising interpretations of several Christmas classics along with stellar originals ("Magical DecorAsians") combine to create a rare New Age holiday gem. There is an intelligence and instinctiveness about these pieces, for Paul is a composer and producer who knows how to please, just where to place a tinkling bell tone or a wood flute timbre in ways that are thrilling and original. The dripping faucet effect in "Oh, Little Town of Bethlehem" plunks out the melody over mandolins and ghostly choir. His style is happily eclectic, bringing together simple melodies, intriguing timbres, and rhythmic and textural influences that span from ethnic and pop to classical. New

> **David Paul Productions**
> PO Box 8550
> JAF Station
> New York, NY 10116
> *NOEL COSMIQUE*: CS $11.95

Age, techno, world and space music influences can all be heard on this work, as well. A variety of music flavors, chilling winter winds and church chimes, and unlikely meters show the uncanny interpretational skills of a film composer, in this case portraying the classic Christmas tales. Included: "We Three Kings," "Good King Wenceslaus," and "What Child Is This?"

Noel Cosmique

David Paul

Describe your music and what you do. I work in the realm of electronic music. I have a small recording studio with computers and synthesizers, and I compose in this high-tech environment. My music is instrumental rather than vocal, and I perform, compose, arrange and record all the parts. I'd say my biggest influences would have to have been other electronic composers like *Jean Michel-Jarre* and *Wendy Carlos.*

How do you hope your music would impact people's lives? Music is very powerful, particularly in a non-verbal context. I feel that music penetrates people very deeply and is just like getting a massage— you don't have to think or busy yourself with logic. I've always intended that my music open up the possibility within my listeners to experience their emotions and express them.

PHIDEAUX: "FRICTION" (1993)

Progressive art rock, Celtic pop. Phideaux Xavier has performed in the New York area since the 80's when he fronted punk/pop combo, *Sally Dick & Jane.* Early 1990 saw the birth of *The SunMachine*, a sextet consisting of guitar, bass, percussion, flute, violin, cello with three strong singers besides Xavier, whose boyish exuberance and soulful intensity create one irresistible package. This is the most engaging work to come along in years! The full promise of *Sgt. Pepper's* comes to fruition on this masterwork by an important new artist. The Celtic pop poetry and art rock pieces cast a beautiful, dreamlike spell that charms and disorients at the same time. The surrealistic imagery and elaborate introductions create a strangely unified whole, though the pieces career stylistically from psychedelic pop to urban dance to dance/pop and sensitive ballads. The focus of these songs is sex, secrets and the supernatural. "Lights, Camera, Friction" obsesses about obsession with sexual paraphernalia. At times,

Phideaux Xavier
c/o Bloodfish Music
172 East 4th Street, #7E
New York, NY 10009
"FRICTION": CS $15...CD $15

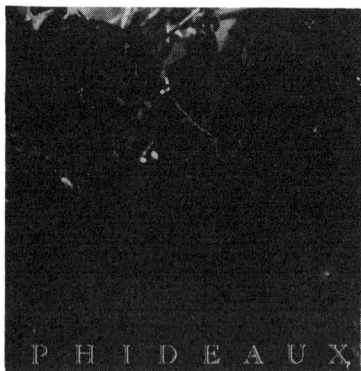

Phideaux sounds uncannily like *Pet Shop Boys' Neil Tennant , Howard Jones* or especially *Al Stewart*, although his musical realizations owe more to progressive rock groups like *Yes, Pink Floyd* and *Electric Light Orchestra*. Through a dense production haze you can smell the sandalwood incense smoke. Both cassette and CD come with a gorgeous full-color 24-page booklet lavishly illustrated with beautiful art and photographs from various members of the community who have created visual interpretations for the songs. As paisley and purple as *Prince*, as schizophrenic an album as the *White Album*, Phideaux puts you in an exquisite trance with these hypnotic spells of music using swirling harmonies, storms of cellos and shimmering guitars. Potent stuff, man. So potent, there ought to be a Hotline for people who trip out on this album. "Hello, 1-800-PHIDEAUX? I'm so smashed on this music I don't even know where I am!" As for me, when I get high on this album, PLEASE...don't talk me down.

ELLIOT PILSHAW AND LORIN SKLAMBERG: BENDING THE RULES (1982)

Elliot Pilshaw has been recording as an out gay musician since his debut release in 1982. He is co-founder of *The Flirtations* (see listing), an original cast member of *Tom Wilson Weinberg's Ten Percent Review*, and founder of *Sons & Lovers*, a new gay a cappella quintet. His debut release has a fresh sound for a work that was recorded twelve years ago! That just goes to prove that there's something timeless about Pilshaw. On *Bending The Rules*, Sklamberg and Pilshaw combine musical excellence with social awareness to give us all yet another means to celebrate and affirm the beauty and validity of our lifestyle. Covers include "Millwork" (*James Taylor*), "Something About The Women" (*Holly Near*), and a remarkably moving interpretation of *Kristin Lem's* "How Nice." (See listing on *Lems*).

Elliot   Lorin
Pilshaw & Sklamberg

BENDING THE RULES

ELLIOT PILSHAW: NATIVE TONGUE (1984)

Folk/ethnic. Alongside his work in the larger gay community, Pilshaw has been especially active in the Jewish gay and lesbian community. He has performed at the *International Conferences of Gay and Lesbian Jews*, traveled and performed extensively throughout Israel, and is currently a cantor at *Congregation Beth Simchat Torah*, New York's gay and lesbian synagogue. This release is a collection of twelve hauntingly beautiful songs by some of Israel's most well-known contemporary songwriters, including *Shalom Hanoch, Yehudit Ravitz* and *David Broza*. With its elegant simplicity, beautiful harmonies and warm acoustic sound, *Native Tongue* will delight the ears of both Hebrew and non-Hebrew speaking listeners. Titles include: "Etz Ha-alon," "Ein-Gedi," and "Shir Ha-Emek."

ELLIOT PILSHAW: FEELS LIKE HOME (1986)

Pop, vocal/piano. Teamed with *John Bucchino* and engaging material, Pilshaw delivers an album that finds its way home into the heart. He covers "exclusively gay" songwriters like *Bucchino, Holly Near, Willie Sordillo, Gary Lapow,* and *Noel Coward* (a love song to a sailor), among others in this warm and satisfying set. Weaving together pop, jazz, folk and Broadway musical styles, Pilshaw has delivered an album of songs that glow with the goodness of gay love, life and friendship. Provocative lyrics, dazzling piano arrangements, and Pilshaw's breathtaking vocals combine to make this album a landmark of gay men's cultural expression. And it has the romantic effect of a roaring fireplace on a sub-zero winter's night. He sings of liberation without blaming or apologizing, informed by pride and a spirited political intelligence, and *John Bucchino* provides lush and elegant piano accompaniment.

How does one create a political statement with an album of love songs? Most of the songs on this album are about gay people, though they could be about anyone who has ever loved another human being deeply. And anyone whose efforts to love that human being have been met with legally-sanctioned discrimination, physical violence, and ostracization from family and friends. In the past few decades, gay people have

Elliot Pilshaw
PO Box 021616
Brooklyn, NY 11201
BENDING THE RULES: CS $6.50
NATIVE TONGUE: CS $12.73

faced all of these with courage and determination, and with increasing success at overcoming them all. That success is marked by the nature of these songs in that they are love songs simple and glowing, not strident and defensive. Instead of stretching to prove the okay-ness of gayness, these songs move on to find the truly human beauty of same-sex closeness and commitment. To find the truly human, universal aspects of gay love is to put same-sex closeness and commitment back into the mainstream of human affairs. By delighting in a smile, in the feel of an embrace, in asking for help and coming

> **Ladyslipper, Inc.**
> PO Box 3124-R
> Durham, NC 27715
> 1-800-634-6044
> *FEELS LIKE HOME*: CS $12.73

through, these songs look beyond gay oppression and reactive responses to it, finding the essence of gay love: people doing their very best to love each other well.

QUEER CONSCIENCE: IT'S A QUEER NATION (1992)

Pop. QueerCon's debut features militantly queer pop songs from Rick Cresswell and gang that bounce along happily in bubble-gum groovy, sixties melodies and arrangements. Cresswell has a muscular tenor that calls to mind *Harry Chapin,* and he uses it to put over songs of defiance that deal with shame, rejection, societal indifference, and self-acceptance. This hard-hitting release features memorable titles and concepts: "In Your Face," "Sex Is Sex," "Gonna Eat My Way To Heaven" (wanna guess what's on his plate?), and "Queerly Beloved" (a wedding song). While the sound may not seem slick or professionally polished to some ears, the raw edges, emotion and heart pull off this project in a fitting manner, and the group hammers home their agenda with amazing grace. There is the definite feel of the an early 70's sound at work here as well, especially that of the power group *Chicago* in their hey-day.

QUEER CONSCIENCE WITH RICK CRESSWELL: BACK TO THE OTHER WORLD? (1993)

Pop. A community activist along with his husband, Rick Cresswell is compelled to get at the greater truths of our struggle for human rights. The couple received a lot of press in 1991 when they participated in a "visibility action" at Boston's *Stocks and Bonds* bar. In that action, the two were attacked by a uniformed Boston police officer because the couple refused to stop kissing each other. On QueerCon's latest release, Cresswell's supple tenor complements the forthright, unflinching lyrics with gentler determination than on the group's debut. Queer Conscience is committed to pushing a blatantly direct queer agenda with such songs as "Telling Someone" and "The Ballad of Harvey Milk." In "OUTside Information," Cresswell sings about the need to be obviously and visibly queer. While less melodically focused, this album has a more polished sound than the group's debut, and again features those irresistibly bouncy 60's arrangements that rescue the release from heavy handedness. With blunt and bruisingly political songs, and a particularly striking album cover collage, this collection will make you want to march.

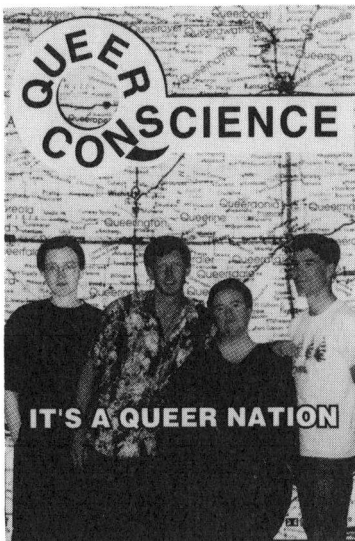

What is the Queer Conscience philosophy? Through the Queer Conscience line of recordings we try to provide recognizable queer music in a variety of styles to increase accessibility instead of censoring ourselves. We are committed to writing about issues that need to be addressed, and then going as far as we can with them. I hope that people will think about the subject matter of our songs, and that they will lead to discussion as well as promoting feelings of pride about who we are.

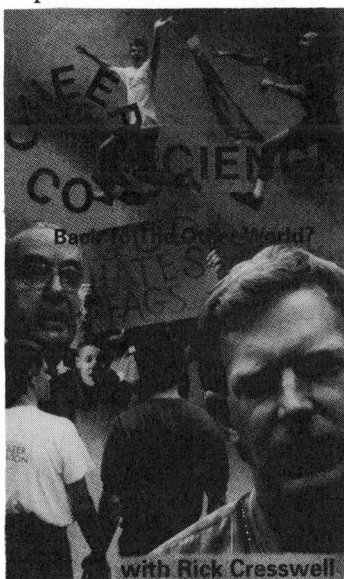

You have a very specific definition of gay music. In my definition, queer music must be obviously queer because our own self-esteem has always been a problem in the community. The more you hear the word gay, the better it sounds.

How did you become a gay musician? I got into it solely for the purpose of providing some of the missing pieces in our culture. Even though many books have been written about the gay experience, very little had been done in music, so I wanted to help start a trend that others (the more the better) would keep alive.

How would you like to see gay music develop? I would like the public to someday be very used to hearing specifically gay music on the radio. I would like gay bars to someday

Scream Sync Production
137 Hollett Street
Scituate, MA 02066-2036
IT'S A QUEER NATION: CS $12.25
BACK TO THE OTHER WORLD: CS $12.25...CD $17

start playing queer music, which in my experience is something that they have not been interested in doing; I think the future of gay pop music lies completely on the gay community, and if we demand music about our lives and not the usual 100% straight music we currently get, then radio stations would naturally comply. However, so far we haven't demanded anything. Hopefully, that will change.

THE RHYTHM METHOD: THE RHYTHM METHOD (1993)

A cappella. The Rhythm Method is a tight lesbian a cappella quartet working out of the Denver area. The groups performs a wide range of music from originals to covers, be-bop and country to traditionals, barbershop and contemporary popular music. And they are a delight! Although they are a new recording act, the group has appeared in concert with *The Flirtations* (see listing), at *Wiminfest* with a cadre of nationally known artists, at the *Gay & Lesbian Chorus Association*'s annual gathering and as the special guests of the *San Francisco Gay & Lesbian Chorus* at *Pride Concert 93.* These gifted women use their incredible voices to weave some intricate vocal arrangements that are simply beyond belief. "The Way You Do," "Haley, Come Down," and "29 Ways" are simply astounding. "You Ain't Thinking About Me" will leave you weak. A feast for the ears!

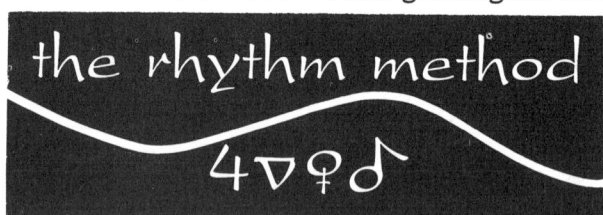

How do you define gay and lesbian music? It is music that reflects our truth, and that validates our experiences as lesbians. It is music that we can sing along with without changing any of the words.

Why do you think is it important to be out as recording artists? To disguise our music in any way would be to disguise ourselves, to devalue ourselves. All four of us are out lesbians at work and in other areas of our lives, so we are not afraid of being out in the entertainment field. It's also important that we show members of the community that we all feel a sense of pride in who we are, and that being lesbian is nothing that needs to be spoken or sung *around,* but can be dealt with directly.

The Rhythm Method
1630 30th Street, #193
Boulder, CO 80301
THE RHYTHM METHOD: CS $12...CD $17

RICK ROBERTSON: SIX (1993)

Alternative rock/pop. These six songs are the result of two unique musical collaborations, and both succeed brilliantly at exploring the farther fringes of alternative pop driven by synthesizer technology, detached alienation, and the longings of a man in limbo. Robertson is blessed with a voice that was made to be recorded, and a gift for writing terrific lyrics that lock into the mood of the musical settings. The sound of this release calls to mind *The Cure, New Order,* and *Depeche Mode.* The moody "For Saturday" is a stand-out smash, but also check out the *Rob Costin* collaborations, "Magnificent Man," "The Lover's Tent," and "Carry Me." (*Costin* himself is an exciting writer and performer of stunning power now at work on his own debut album). The ease, power and poetic language of this release are pure genius, and Robertson may just be our own little psychedelic-era *Bob Dylan,* a poet and prophet of queerdom. **How would you characterize you music?** I sing melodic modern rock; melancholy, spacy, a bit dark, haunting, experienced. Being gay, I sometimes wonder about the audience; mostly I perform in front of gay audiences, but the show has gone over very well in front of straight crowds also.

RICK ROBERTSON

Who are some of your personal influences? *David Bowie, Roxy Music, Joni Mitchell, Patti Smith, Jacques Brel, Joy Division.*

What influence has music had on your life? Music has been a constant companion since I was about 9 years old and got my first transistor radio. Music has been a friend when none were present, a mirror for hopes, fears, triumphs and disappointments. Not everyone listens this way; hopefully some will find my music their "friend" and companion.

Rick Robertson
28 Burwood Road
Toronto, Ontario
Canada M9B 2W5
SIX: CS $9

What is your approach to gay music? If I'm doing a song about a "he," I don't make it "she" (unless in the queenie sense). The mainstream bores and repulses me, and even if my music isn't all that "gay," I have no interest in being part of the mainstream right now.

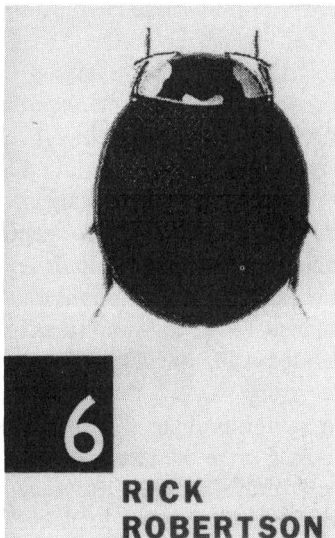

ROMANOVSKY & PHILLIPS: I THOUGHT YOU'D BE TALLER (1984)

Pop/rock. Romanovsky & Phillips (R&P) are easily the most popular out-of-the-closet singing duo in history. Having toured extensively in the U.S., Canada and Australia, R&P have earned the title of "Ambassadors of Homosexuality." Prolific and long-standing members of the gay music community, R&P have a hysterically comic bent on contemporary gay life. Each of their albums is also peppered with beautifully romantic ballads and sensitive and politically impassioned numbers that give their releases exhilarating balance. Fifties doo-wop parodies with silly kazoo solos don't seem out of place beside poignant ballads in the musical world of R&P. As the most successful gay group in the history of our community, R&P have been on the forefront of gay entertainment for over a decade. Since gay people love to hear about nothing more than themselves, these two brilliant young men write about what we couldn't possibly hear enough about, our favorite subject: ourselves. And, why not? Gay people have been so invisibilized in the media and American society, it's about time we Hear Queer. Who can resist: "Closet Case," "I Can Have Attitude," and "She Has A Thing For Men Who Love Men"? This album was the folky beginning of the dynastic duo, and reflects the sound they honed in their humble, hummable beginnings as a San Francisco folk duo in the early 80's. As such, it showcases the wonderful harmony vocal arrangements of their two distinctive voices, and contains their most naive, but always charming material.

ROMANOVSKY & PHILLIPS: TROUBLE IN PARADISE (1986)

Pop/rock. Every song this duo writes becomes an instant community classic. Expertly tuned into gay fascinations and foibles, R&P nail the issues in love and politics right on the head. On their second release, they were teamed for the first time with producer *Teresa Trull* (Ms. Trull went on to produce *Ron Romanovsky's* 1992 solo album—see listing), who utilized keyboards, drums, sax...a full production treatment, and a song cycle blending mightily R&P's comic takes and romantic killers. More classics: "What Kind Of Self-Respecting Faggot Am I?," "Wimp," "Homophobia," "Must've Been Drunk," "The Answering Machine Song," and "Don't Use Your Penis For A Brain." This "sounds" like a hit album should sound, and is probably their best-known work. With *Trouble In Paradise*, they grew leaps and bounds above their auspicious debut, and became international gay pop stars.

ROMANOVSKY & PHILLIPS: EMOTIONAL ROLLERCOASTER (1988)

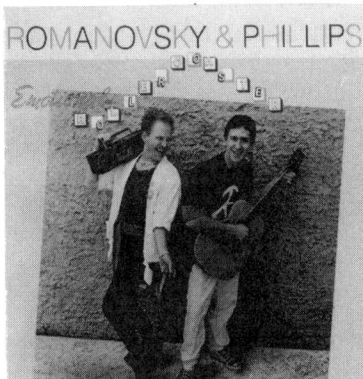

Pop/rock. On the third album they changed the formula a little bit and captured the crazy cabaret ambience of their live performances, leaning toward vaudeville. But it's the vaudeville treatment given this album that nearly covers up the fact that R&P have written the most incisive and brilliantly observed lyrics of their career. Classics: "The Sodomy Song," "Give Me A Homosexual," "My Mother's Clothes" and "I've Created A Monster."

ROMANOVSKY & PHILLIPS: BE POLITICAL, NOT POLITE (1991)

Pop/rock. It was three years before R&P managed a follow-up to their record three releases of blatant gay pop music. In the meantime they had become the most successful, beloved and prolific group in the history of gay music. This was a significant event in Pop Music history as well as gay pop. The couple also broke up amicably during 1990, deciding to continue recording and performing together. And lucky for us! *Political* is the best album of their career to date, produced with perfect restraint by *John Bucchino* with R&P. This album is a feast of R&P at the top of their form. Remember: *Fleetwood Mac* recorded *Rumours,* one of the best selling albums of all time, while the two couples in the group were divorcing. Out of pain, it seems, art thrives. Their latest release balances a little heavily on the political side, as the title suggests, but the message is handled with typical R&P deftness. Packed with 15 songs of love,

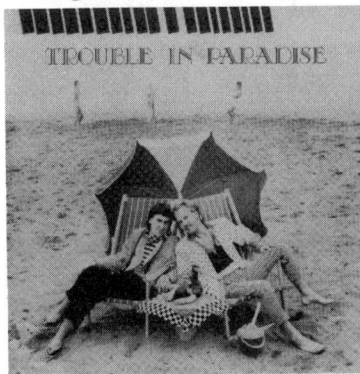

anger, politics and hope, the duo covers a wide range of subjects from lesbian/gay parents to lesbian/gay teachers, from surviving AIDS to surviving dating. The stellar line-up of guest vocalists include *Holly Near, Alix Dobkin (see listing), Phranc,* and *Michael Callen (see listing).* As always, the harmonies are terrific. Classics include: "Tango Indigesto," "Queers In The Closet," "When Heterosexism Strikes" and "OH NO I'm In Love (With My Therapist)."

RON ROMANOVSKY: HOPEFUL ROMANTIC (1992)

Pop/rock. For his solo effort, Romanovsky tapped *Teresa Trull* to produce, and the team has delivered one of the best gay albums in years. The music is mostly upbeat and covers a wide variety of musical styles woven together with some of Romanovsky's best vocals ever. At his tenderest, he evokes *Don McLean*, but in the world of Ron Romanovsky, a polka party never seems out of place. As a solo artist, Romanovsky ventures into new territory with the *Gershwin*-esque "A Measure of Sadness," the rock and roll riffs of "The Perfect Crime," and the seductive cabaret-blues of "Baby Take Advantage of Me." This is his most mature writing and the most supple production settings of his work yet. "Battle Scars" bubbles with a samba beat driven by a *Dire Straits* guitar sound. The album is a one man variety songwriting showcase, and his most polished sound and sophisticated songwriting to date. Ron Romanovsky is a superb ambassador of homosexuality, and this is the album of his career.

Describe Romanovsky & Phillips in your own words! RON: If my music could be described or categorized, the record stores would know what bin to put R&P in. As it is, you might find us under "Vocals" because our harmonies have been compared to *Simon & Garfunkel, The Roches*, and the *Indigo Girls.* You might find us under "Comedy" because we've been compared to the *Smothers Brothers.* You might find us under "Women's Music" because some of our work is politically parallel to lesbian pioneers like *Meg Christian* and *Alix Dobkin (see listing)*, and because there is no bin for "Gay Men's Music." Or you might find us under "Folk" because of our acoustic tendencies. All of these categories describe some aspect of our work, but individually they are extremely limiting. Much of our work is satirical, much of it is not. All of it paints a picture or tells a story. PAUL: Trying to define our musical style is difficult. Do we do folk, pop, cabaret, show tunes, ballads, novelty songs, anthems, acoustic rock? Yes, and we also utilize musical styles from the 40's, 50's and 60's, not to mention Latin rhythmic styles. Our repetoire does not fit neatly into one genre, making it all that much more unique. As to what we do, I'd say that we perform

original music and comedy which brings illumination and education, definition and demystification, insight and amusement, challenge and healing to our own lives and hopefully to the lives of others as well. And we have lots of fun doing it.

What's it like having had such a long and successful career as out gay performers and recording artists? RON: If you have made a choice to be out as an artist, that is a political choice. It means you are an activist as well as an artist, which carries with it a certain amount of responsibility. I don't feel like I speak for all gay and lesbian people, but I know that many non-gay people think I do, and this is something I try to keep in mind. PAUL: The down side is that there are times when I'd much rather be involved in my creative process than battling homophobia and fighting for my basic civil rights. But the benefits certainly outweigh the drawbacks.

How has music impacted your lives and how do you hope your music will impact other people's lives? RON: Listening to music was how I survived childhood and adolescence; I started buying records when I was six. Music provided an escape, solace, comfort, inspiration, and it gave me hope that the world was more beautiful than I had so far been shown. Listening to great music that you really love, whether it's *Janis Joplin* or *Mozart*, can be a spiritual experience. I think at its best, music heals people by reminding them of beauty and love. PAUL: I believe that no social or political movement can fully succeed without its own cultural and artistic expression. The lesbian and gay movement is no exception. Music can heal, inspire, incite, challenge and unify. I hope in some small way (and maybe in some BIG way!) our music can accomplish some or all of those things.

What is your definition of gay music? RON: My (narrow) definition of gay and lesbian music is music that unmistakably discusses experiences and feelings that are unique to being gay and lesbian.

Why have you chosen to do gay music? RON: It's what I do best and I believe that it is the best way for me to make a contribution to the world. It was not a difficult choice. PAUL: I found role models in the likes of

Fresh Fruit Records
369 Montezuma #209
Santa Fe, NM 87501
1-800-473-7848
I THOUGHT YOU'D BE TALLER: CS $13...CD $18
TROUBLE IN PARADISE: CS $13...CD $18
EMOTIONAL ROLLERCOASTER: CS $13...CD $18
BE POLITICAL, NOT POLITE: CS $15...CD $19
HOPEFUL ROMANTIC: CS $13...CD $18

Holly Near, Margie Adam (see listing) and *Charlie Murphy,* who were singing music which was relevant to my life. And there is a part of me that wants to show other young gay men and lesbians that they can be successful and true to themselves at the same time.

What is your vision of gay music? RON: I don't have a vision for gay music, but I hope that one day being gay and lesbian is such a non-issue that there will be less of a need for songs that deal specifically with being gay. As far as gay pop music, I think there will be songs on the charts with gay content as soon as record companies smell money and figure out how to market it. I don't know how much longer that will take.

TOMMIE SAELI: HELLO (1993)

Alternative rock / glam rock. This is one of the coolest discs of the year, in *or* out of the mainstream! Saeli is a retro-rocker, best known as the host of cable's *Gay Dating Game.* The crunchy sound of this disc is a throwback to the early 70's glam rock of gender-benders *David Bowie* and *T. Rex*: heavy drumming, handclaps and football cheer choruses. It's a hard sound with no guitars, just layers of rock cello and cathedral organ. With the exception of the drumming, the album is a one man tour de force. The rock cello-wielding Saeli (a former go-go dancer at NYC's *Pyramid Club*) is a hot muscled Italian boy in a pink glitter metallic suit and feather boa, who offsets the sexy *Billy Idol* growl of his voice with a *Yoko Ono*-like falsetto that accompanies him in unison on many of the songs. With dazzlingly mind bending lyrics that blend myth, fantasy and magic, Saeli weaves a psychedelic spell once he gets that *Marc Bolan* groove going. "Rock & Roll Queen" evokes *Elton John*'s ripping "Saturday Night's Alright For Fighting." "Michaelangelo Irreducible" is a Motown (*Supremes*...surprised?) take-off. "Lady Of The Well" sports a *Moody Blues* harpsichord. Take the savage sweetness of *John Lennon*, add the guts of *David Bowie*, the flash fame of *Nirvana*, the magic of *Sigfried and Roy* and shake...don't stir. Say hello!

How would you describe your project? I am the "gay glitter rock vocalist/cellist." My CD is a solo project, but I recently put a band together and am performing locally in the NYC area.

It's safe to say that your sound hearkens back to the glam-rock era. My music is influenced by early 70's glam sounds. I really enjoy bands like *T.Rex, Slade* and *Gary Glitter.*

Tommie Saeli
Howling Wolf Records
75 2nd Avenue, #2
New York, NY 10003
HELLO: CD $15

How has music affected your life? I think music is a secret language of emotions. It transcends time and space. Music is the only art form able to surreptitiously change your mood. I find it a very subtle but powerful way to influence opinions.

How do you define gay music? There is no such thing as "gay" music. Conversely, there is no such thing as "straight" music. I hope people would just be more open to "music."

Your lyrics are not overtly gay. Why have you chosen to identify with gay pop? However self-delusional it may be, I see myself pursuing a mainstream career. That doesn't mean I'm afraid to say I'm a fag. Being gay is great and people should be more tolerant. I want to perform for audiences that are mixed. Singing for an all-gay audience is like preaching to the converted.

What is your vision of gay music? I want people to be more tolerant and accepting of everyone. I hope people would enjoy my music not just because I'm gay, but because they like it. We know that being gay isn't a choice; it's genetic. With that in mind, I don't seek special treatment for a biological fact. It's like asking people to like me because I have green eyes.

ANNE SEALE: SEX FOR BREAKFAST (1991)

Pop/comedy. Anne Seale is a one-woman *Romanovsky & Phillips* (see listing), that is to say a stand-up singer/comedienne. Her debut release is frankly lesbian, mostly humorous, and very affirming of the homosexual experience. The *Carmen Miranda* take of the title track is hilarious, as is her loving tribute to "Body Hair." The tracks are a little...loungy, but somehow complement Seale's deadpan delivery. The overall effect is a tape that careens from ultra-hip to goofily offbeat, *Sandy Dennis* in *David Lynch* land, or *Mary Martin* on the planet Lesbos. Either way, it's worth a listen for "Your Women's Bookstore," "Women-Womyn-Wimmin" ("I'm a liberated female / and I want to see us grow / but exactly how to spell us / I don't know!") and "I Get A Rash

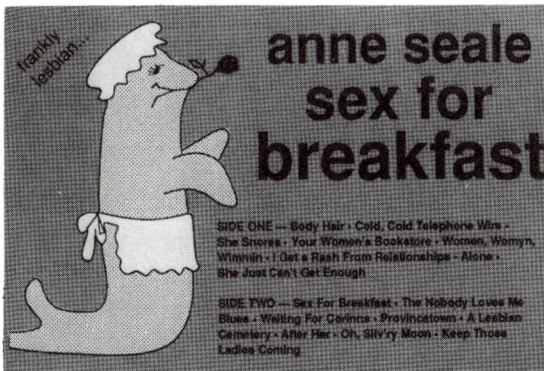

anne seale
sex for
breakfast

SIDE ONE — Body Hair · Cold, Cold Telephone Wire · She Snores · Your Women's Bookstore · Women, Womyn, Wimmin · I Get a Rash From Relationships · Alone · She Just Can't Get Enough

SIDE TWO — Sex For Breakfast · The Nobody Loves Me Blues · Waiting For Corinne · Provincetown · A Lesbian Cemetery · After Her · Oh, Silv'ry Moon · Keep Those Ladies Coming

From Relationships." The album also contains a heart-wrenching ballad that reveals true tenderness and depth, "After Her." Twisted, demented and disarmingly real, this release reflects the joys and kinks of lesbian living.

Who are some of your personal artistic influences? *Rodgers & Hammerstein, Lerner & Lowe, Sondheim.* All the 30's, 40's and early 50's lyricists. *Alan Sherman, Alix Dobkin* (see listing), *Lea Delaria,* and all my lovers and friends.

How has music changed your life? Music has been a thread running

> **Anne Seale**
> Wildwater Records
> PO Box 56
> Webster, NY 14580-0056
> *SEX FOR BREAKFAST*: CS $12

throughout my life, providing color, excitement and purpose. Music can run the gamut from diversion to a catalystic agent, and often has changed people's lives emotionally, politically and even physically (aerobics!). I hope my music will bring laughter, pride and a sense of belonging to my listeners.

How do you define gay/lesbian music? In my opinion, it should relate to the lesbian and gay experience. Just being written by a gay/lesbian person is not enough. It should address issues specific to our world view and lives.

JOSEPH VICTOR SIEGER: SELF-PORTRAIT, 1993 (1993)

Synth/pop/alternative. Absolutely uncompromising, without-a-net performance of over the edge, self-ghettoized, gay-sex-obsessed material. PyschoSemiPornographic music for the groin, this disk reeks of *RUSH*, leather and mansweat. The album is an incredibly hot journey into the super sexual psyche of master Sieger, whose voice ranges from pleasing to deranged, vulnerable warble to menacing squeak. This release combines an 80's retro synth-pop sound with touches of 90's techno, and freely mixes rap with balladry, consistently exhibiting an experimental electronic edge. Subversive the way a *Prince* album can be, *Self-Portrait* features twenty spare but hypnotic grooves that drive you into a frenzy the way only the Purple One can do. But *Prince* never talked dirty like this! In "I'm A Ghost," Sieger walks the "darkened halls, haunting the backrooms and the bathroom stalls." Sizzling tracks include: "Top Rap," "Sun & Steel," "Master," and "We Will Rise." His dance hall cover of the *Marlene Dietrich* classic "Boys In The Backroom" ("See what the boys in the backroom will have / and tell them I died of the same") takes on new resonance. The album also contains a brave a cappella reading of *Village People*'s "San Francisco (You Got Me)." This is the great dance underground album of the year: one for the crotch. A brilliant independent release, he *will* excite you.

JOSEPH VICTOR SIEGER ■ SELF-PORTRAIT, 1993

Describe your music. I'm an electronic musician, working with synth-pop. Everything I do is computer-based so I guess that makes me a digital artist— maybe a virtual performer—since I rely so heavily on sequencing and don't have any real musical chops of my own in terms of playing. But that's okay. I

look at the final product as the work of art and am less concerned with how it was arrived at. How it sounds is all that matters to me.
Who are some of your personal artistic influences? *Andy Warhol, Robert Mapplethorpe* and *Rip Colt.* I took the art-school route through painting, photography and filmmaking to arrive at music. I've always been interested in the expression of the masculine ideal in the arts, but always with a definite sense of style that

> **Siegerwerke, Inc.**
> PO Box 14348
> San Francisco, CA 94114-0348
> *SELF-PORTRAIT 1993*: CD...$20
> (Please sign and state that you are 21 years of age.)

isn't necessarily considered masculine in and of itself. Musically, I greatly admire *Laurie Anderson, Brian Eno, Annie Lennox* and *Morrissey,* among many others. Actually, I'm a huge music fan and collector. Sometimes I joke that I'm doing all this just to meet *Morrissey.*
How has music impacted your life? *Bowie* as *Ziggy Stardust* helped me find myself. I found *Patti Smith's Horses* totally liberating. When I heard *Kraftwerk's Trans-Europe Express* (at the baths, coincidentally), I came to the realization that music was what I wanted to do and so I bought a synthesizer and formed a band with my best friend.
What are you trying to accomplish with your music? I'm basically exploring and expressing my own self in hopes that other people might find things in me that are like them. I'm interested in showing how people are alike. I know my work is shocking to some people but it really is perfectly natural to my experience and, more than anything, that's what I hope to be: natural. However, I do see the irony in choosing an artificial medium to express my naturalness.
How do you define gay music? I would say that gay music is music by gay artists dealing with gay themes. Not everything I do is gay music because my homosexuality isn't relevant to every theme I explore. But it does form the bulk of my work to this point so that would make me a gay musician.
What do you think lies ahead for gay music? I see gay people expressing themselves without apology and without self-pity and with pride in who we are and where we've been. The last thing I want to see is assimilation and the loss of a separate gay identity and culture. We shouldn't be trying to be more like straight society. They should be trying to be more like us!

FRED SMALL: HEART OF THE APPALOOSA (1983)
Folk/pop. Recognized as one of the most politically committed artists on the acoustic music scene, Fred Small practices topical songwriting in the tradition of *Phil Ochs, Woody Guthrie* and *Tom Paxton.* Powerful, affecting and inviting, Small's songs illumine the goodness and courage of all kinds of

FRED SMALL

The Heart of the Appaloosa

people faced with adversity. His music is naturally insightful, literate and thought-provoking, revealing the pop social conscience of *Bruce Cockburn*. Educated as an attorney, Small gave up his law practice in 1980 to pursue a career in music full-time, and has performed throughout the United States and all over the world, bringing his inspirational message to thousands. Small is carrying the torch of committed social singers and shines his light on progressive political messages: the environment, gay and lesbian issues, feminism, nuclear disarmament, civil rights for women and people with disabilities, global warming—you name it, and Small sings about it. He has a journalist's eye, and thankfully avoids tying up his lyrics with platitudes or placard-sized slogans.

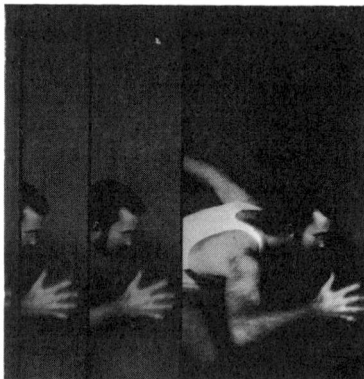

FRED SMALL: NO LIMIT (1985)
Folk/bluegrass. Small returned with a strong follow-up in 1985. Insightful standouts include: "Big Italian Rose" and "Leslie Is Different." This album introduced the much-covered classic "Everything Possible," a child's lullaby promoting acceptance, self-love, and tolerance for gays and lesbians; your basic three-minute Rainbow Curriculum.

FRED SMALL: I WILL STAND FAST (1988)
Folk/rock. On what is perhaps his best-known album, a duet with *Mary-Chapin Carpenter* pairs him with a spiritual sister and fellow traveler, and

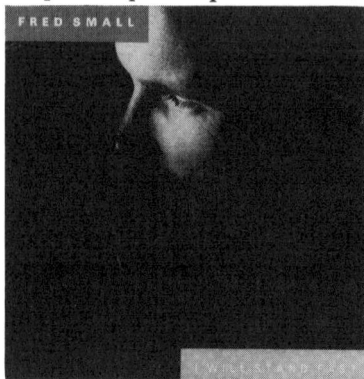

someone who mines a similar folk/country/rock crossover sound mixed with social sensibility, though *Carpenter*'s tends more toward the romantic gesture and Small's toward grander sociopolitical issues. Indeed, conflicts on the world stage are the topics of quite a number of songs here, including Arab-Israeli, South Africa's apartheid, and Russo-American. The stand-out here is the sweet, childlike classic "If I Were A Moose" ("...and you were a cow / would you love me anyhow?") "Scott And Jamie" deals with the true story of two parents whose adoptive rights were reversed when it was discovered that the two fathers were gay lovers. World conflict, and issues of blood and war make for entertainment that is extremely challenging on this transitional release. Small obviously had a lot on his mind that he needed to get across, but all this aggression thankfully led to his best work (see below).

FRED SMALL: JAGUAR (1991)
Rock/pop/folk. Fred Small is at his most engaging on this forthright studio release. He is given the most powerful production yet, and he uses that to break new ground here. Small writes with a renewed focus, songs that deserve the muscular settings of these pieces and he carries them off with command. He has never sounded so good! Small mines quite a potent combination of material: environmentalism, longing for a better world, romantic regret, and issues of child sexual abuse and incest. Throughout his career, Small has evolved his sound from raw folkie to one more polished and mainstream that suits him better. On *Jaguar*, you get the impression that Small identifies with the endangered animal, because the balance of these songs are about loss of love and betray a bitterness, a sadness, a turning inward. The music crackles on this disc (check out the reggae beat of "Gravity"), and there is an edgy buoyancy to his vocals that adds just the right dramatic touches to the material. This is an album with hard edges, and ironically, his most impressive studio work to date.

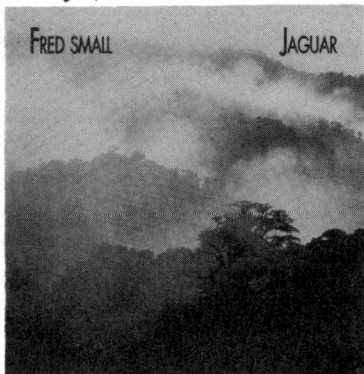

FRED SMALL: EVERYTHING POSSIBLE (1993)
Folk/pop. This live album showcases the warmth, fun and electricity of Fred Small in concert, and the audiences are obviously having a great time. The live format provides a splendid opportunity to present the best material from his four studio albums, as well as terrific new tunes. Fred is so smart, so socially aware, with such a highly developed intellect and gifted with such grace, tolerance and loving, and not handicapped at all by being straight, that he should be the poster boy for The Model Man. Fred Small speaks to the best in us, to the child in us unspoiled by fear and prejudice. This is the man I want the children of this country listening to and idolizing. Small is a role model who embodies peace, love, intelligence, ecology, and compassion for all men. He deserves the widest possible audience for his work; the more folks who embrace Fred Small, the better off this planet will be. He's more huggable than

that idiotic purple dinosaur *Barney*, and eons more relevant. Standouts on an album of standouts include: "I Want A Hug," "Friends First," "Hot Frogs On The Loose," "Marine's Lament (or The Pink Peril)," and "Everything Possible." This is a terrific introduction to Fred Small at his most accessible, and features some of his most endearing songs.

How do you describe what you do? I am an

Small Potatoes
PO Box 765
Acton, MA 01720
1-800-788-6043
HEART OF THE APPALOOSA: CS $13...CD $18
NO LIMIT: CS $13...CD $18
I WILL STAND FAST: CS $13...CD $18
JAGUAR: CS $13...CD $18
EVERYTHING POSSIBLE: CS $13...CD $18

activist singer/songwriter. Intended to heal and empower, my songs address many liberation issues, including gay rights. *The Flirtations* (see listing) have brought my lullaby "Everything Possible" to gay audiences around the world.

Who would you number as personal artistic influences? My major influences have been *Pete Seeger, Tom Paxton, Phil Ochs, Stan Rogers,* and *Holly Near.* The purpose of my songs is to move people emotionally, intellectually, and spiritually, and to empower them to change themselves and the world.

You have come out as an avowed heterosexual. Why have you chosen to list your work in the GAY MUSIC GUIDE? As a heterosexual, I chose for many years not to discuss my sexual orientation onstage so as not to take advantage of heterosexual privilege. But in light of right-wing backlash against the gay community, I have decided the best strategy for me now is to model straight support for gay rights. At my concerts I encourage heterosexuals in the audience to actively support gay rights.

DOUG STEVENS & THE OUTBAND: OUT IN THE COUNTRY

(1993) *Contemporary country/rock.* The runaway favorite of the year, this pop biography could have been called "Meet Doug Stevens," because Stevens not only writes and sings good songs, he's lived them. The Tupelo, Mississippi native begins with his tale of kissing boy cousins ("Out In The Country") and southern intolerance ("Born In Mississippi"). He then leaves for the big city ("Git While The Gittin's Good"), falls in love ("Sweet Breath of Love"), looks back in anger ("White Trash"), loses his lover when he's diagnosed with HIV ("HIV Blues"), and emerges stronger and renewed of spirit ("Act Up"). This is country rock with the pure reckless excitement of a live set   that sizzles and swings. *Doug Stevens and The Outband* are consistently winning fans in the gay and straight country music communities. In the short time this band has been together they've played *Gracie Mansion, Town Hall* in NYC with *Joan Rivers, The Rainbow Room* at *Rockefeller*

Center, and *The 1993 March On Washington.* There they were seen by 3,000,000 people around the world on *C-SPAN*, and millions more on the *NBC Evening News* affiliates. They have appeared three times on *In The Life*, and have played at many 2-step dances and concerts on the east coast and in the mid-west. This thoroughly entertaining and consistent album is produced with sparkling clarity and punch. The pansexual line-up includes the wicked fiddle work of *John Cordes* and the electrifying lead guitar work of *Desiree*, who has a strong guest spot as lead vocalist on the self-penned "Cactus Country." Mandolin and fiddle accompany the softer selections with lovely lyrics that are pure poetry that speak of the passionate love for men. *The Outband* owes much to country/rock crossover traditions like *Linda Ronstadt, The Eagles* and *Neil Young*. On this debut that is nothing less than a gay music cultural milestone, *The Outband* embodies what the best "country music" should be: rock with an accent.

How did you go from classical training and singing opera to country/western? Initially I began to write songs when I found out I was HIV positive and my lover left me. I thought I could get rid of the pain if I wrote a country/ western song about it.

So your lover didn't believe in standing by his man. No, he cut out, like "You picked a bad time to leave me Lucille."

Have you always wanted to sing? I have been a singer ever since I was five years old, singing *Doris Day's "Que Sera Sera"* with her on the radio, trying to get my voice to match hers perfectly.

Doug Stevens
31-65 29th Street, #A-6
Astoria, NY 11106
OUT IN THE COUNTRY: CS $12.50...CD $17.50

What do you hope to achieve with your music? My purpose is to create country/western music with gay and lesbian lyrics, and to introduce the hetero world to gay and lesbian lives. I love being an out gay performer. Not only am I out, but I am celebrating to the public my ability to be honest. I am saying that being gay is good, that I have nothing to hide, I have something to celebrate and proclaim!

MARSHA STEVENS: FREE TO BE (1991)

Contemporary Christian. Marsha Stevens is a star in the religious community and rightfully so. She's written the hugely popular and widely covered modern hymn, "For Those Tears I Died," and is regarded with the reverence us ordinary mortals reserve for, well, someone we revere. Her classic has been included in almost every church hymnal published since 1972. Marsha came out as a born-again lesbian thirteen years ago and now sings and writes as a ministry to the gay and lesbian Christian community. She is also the mother of two grown children. On her debut release, she offers music and songs that make you feel clean the way listening to *Up With People* did. It's not a sin to admit that you enjoy indulging in gospel rock; it could just put you in touch with you-know-who. She delivers monumental pop/rock melodies and arrangements, and is not in the least heavy-handed in her approach to getting her message across. If you like the clean sound of New Country music divas like *Wynonna* and *Trisha Yearwood*, you'll love Marsha Stevens.

MARSHA STEVENS: THE BEST IS YET TO COME (1992)

Contemporary Christian. Comparisons to *Amy Grant* and *Michael W. Smith* would be too obvious, and anyway Stevens possesses a charm and confidence not found in the mainstream. One listen will make a believer out of you. Every song reaches shattering climaxes of fervor. Witness "Celebrate": "Celebrate our Maker / shatterer of lies / Who in fierce compassion brings into our lives / A strength we never had before / fling wide the closet door / We know for such a time as this / God's people are called forth." If *Whitney Houston* was using her incredible instrument to record anything but bland pop fodder, this is what she might sound like.

Tell me about your path as a lesbian music artist. What I do is contemporary Christian music for the gay community. Having previously toured for nine years (1970-79) in the straight evangelical world, I lost a lot of friends when I came out. I've had people rip a page out of their church hymnals with a song I wrote on it and mail it to me with hate mail. But

BALM Publishing PO Box 1981 Costa Mesa, CA 92628 *FREE TO BE:* CS $11.50 *THE BEST IS YET TO COME:* CS $11.50...CD $16.50 *I STILL HAVE A DREAM:* CS $11.50...CD $16.50 *LIVE IN CONCERT:* VHS Video $21.50

I've been able to reach much more people who could hear a positive message about God's love for them, because they knew my music.

How would you like your music to impact people's lives? I hope my music breaks through the religious rhetoric we've come to hate and talks about our longing to see purpose in our existence and healing for our hearts.

What is gay/lesbian music in your definition? I really like the idea of having a musical genre that speaks specifically to our lives. In this society we are still set apart legally, socially and religiously. As long as that is true, I want to hear music that, even subtly, refers to us: our lives, relationships and struggles.

Why did you decide to come out as a lesbian Christian musician? I love Christian music...the comfort of hymns in my childhood; the searching, yearning songs of freedom as I got older. And even the positive pop of more recent years: *Amy Grant, Garth Brooks, Bette Midler* ("God is watching us..."). Who's writing it for us? I'd like others to have that richness in their lives and I love doing it.

How do you see the future of gay pop music? I hope as we become more vocal and more out with our talents, that our perspective on the world as outcasts, as hidden people, as a group actually defined by our love, becomes as much a part of the musical world as black gospel, Latin music, country, etc.

MARSHA STEVENS: I STILL HAVE A DREAM (1993)

Contemporary Christian. Between the lavish production given these unforgettable songs, and the beautiful devotional sentiment, Marsha Stevens is gaining converts among people who get nervous at the mere mention of the J-word (*Jesus*). Amazingly, Stevens just gets better and better. Outstanding tracks on this release include: "Come Out And Go Forth," "I'm Blessed," the title track, and a remake of her classic, "For Those Tears I Died." If Marsha Stevens is the house band in heaven, even I'll be good! An absolutely spectacular album from start to finish.

Marsha Stevens
Live In Concert

25th Anniversary Edition

MARSHA STEVENS: LIVE IN CONCERT—VHS VIDEO 75 Minutes (1993)

Contemporary Christian. Marsha Stevens uses the concert forum to charm and inspire us with her terrific music and God-given vocal ability, as well as to share her story. And what a story! Stevens is utterly charming, lovable and touching in this truly moving, feel-good video filmed in Los Angeles at the *Metropolitan Community Church.* That she has three albums out on her own *Born Again Lesbian Music (BALM)* label is impressive enough; that her first composition, "For Those Tears I Died" was written at age 16 and is an unqualified international Christian standard is truly remarkable (a miracle?). As a gift to your heart, you owe it to yourself to discover *Marsha Stevens*: she will lift your spirits and bring you a little closer to heaven.

JAN TILLEY: SCARLET LETTER (1993)

Rock/pop. Wow! This out lesbian rock chick will set your ears on fire! If you're passionate about the melodic pop/rock, crunchy guitar hooks, and raw vocals of rock divas like *Debbie Harry* of *Blondie,* and *Joan Jett,* you will love Jan

Tilley! Heavily influenced by glam and punk rock, Tilley started performing professionally in the 70's, at a time when females were unheard of in the rock field. In 1981, she became a founding member of the all-female punk group, *Rude Girls.* More recently, she has formed *OUTcast Productions,* a distribution company for lesbian/gay musicians and women in rock. On the album's title track, which deals with having to hide sexual preferences, she sings "I'm not gonna wear my love for her like a scarlet letter." Great vocal harmonies, throwback arrangements, and lyrical attitude betray a woman who revels in her chosen genre. An amazing debut. Turn it up!

How do you describe your music? I'm a punk rocker (lead guitarist, vocalist and

jan TILLEY
Scarlet Letter

songwriter). I front a six-piece rock band that consists of me and five guys. Being out is the only way for me. I've experienced sexism and homophobia in my career; I even got fired from a club when they found out I was gay, but

these things only drive me harder and make me all the more determined. Anger is a great motivator for me! But, mostly my experiences have been very positive. I've always had a loyal following of gays and straights, males and females.

Who are some of your personal artistic influences? *Blondie, Cheap Trick, Alice Cooper, David Bowie, Suzi Quatro...The Rolling Stones.*

What is your vision of the future of gay pop music? Right now there is so much gay music that it's time to stop pretending it doesn't exist. To me, we should exist very obviously, until our music is accepted and not considered "different" or a big issue.

PUSSY TOURETTE: PUSSY TOURETTE IN HI-FI (1993)

Rock/pop/blues. Profane, shameless trash and of course, a smash hit! With a gift for self-invention, this fiercest of drag divas constructs the myth and legend of Pussy Tourette while simultaneously deconstructing queer misconceptions. This ain't no disco, honey! From the New Orleans *Dr. John* camp of "If I Can't

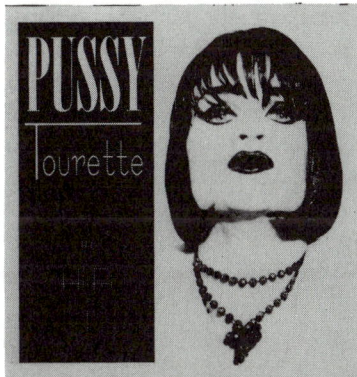

Sell It..." ("...I'm gonna sit back down on it / I ain't about to give it away") to the gritty *Led Zeppelin*-influenced heavy blues of "Free Pussy," it's clear that Ms. Tourette is not the girl next door. Beginning as a go-go dancer in San Francisco's teeming underground scene, Tourette was acclaimed the hottest and sauciest act on the city's cabaret scene when she started singing her original compositions live. Touring nationally has helped her develop nothing less than a fanatical following. Five Tourette songs are featured in *Sex Is*, which won the *Best Gay Film Award* at Berlin's *International Film Festival*. *Pussy Tourette in Hi-Fi* is a mad romp. Along the way, opera divas ponder queerdom, a tribute to cocktail lounge era *Ann Margaret* ("After You"), gold-diggers going into orgasms over "Bracelets," and an infectious twist boogie with the cheer-along chorus of "Phuque my pussy!" This is leagues removed from the smooth disco gloss of crossover drag sister *RuPaul*. Tourette has a streetwise, gritty gift for rock/blues. When combined with her weirdly flanged voice, she can sound as down and dirty as *Prince* at his filthiest. "French Bitch" is an instant queer classic (the video has more slaps per minute than any other music video in history!) Warning: This pussy is no kitten! Hers is a world peopled with cheap hustlers, bitchy supermodels, boys who want to be ladies, and material girls, all set in orbit around ferocious emcee, Pussy Tourette. Bravo, Ms. Tourette redefines what it means to be different. If I'd had any idea that pussy was this good, well...nevermind!

What does your unlimited ambition include? I want to be the first real out queen on *MTV*. Not this *Boy George* pseudo-half drag thing.

TRIBE 8: BY THE TIME WE GET TO COLORADO (1993)

Punk. Thrash metal girls with an in-your-face lesbian political agenda, Tribe 8 is part of the new riot grrrl punk scene which orginated in Seattle, the current hotbed of grunge rock. The two-year-old, all-dyke, San Francisco-based band has been getting a good deal of attention lately stemming from their militant

feminist and queer politics. This six song set evokes the raw aggression of L.A.'s now-defunct seminal punk group *X*, at other times the urgent sexuality of *The Doors,* and the angry rhythmic poetry of *Jim Carroll.* "Lesbophobia" blasts straight girls aghast at being cruised. I play this disc and start slamming into things. Tribe 8 will make you want to mosh. Music as menacing as the cover art.

The Gay Music Guide interviewed Matt Wobensmith, president of the Outpunk record label.

What is the Outpunk label all about? Outpunk, my record label, is the first and only queer punk record label in existence. Thousands of young people nation-wide have access to the out queer music on my label. (See listing for *God Is My Co-Pilot*).

What's your working definition of gay/lesbian music? Bands and performers who are out. Ambiguity is not acceptable, because we don't live in

---

Outpunk
PO Box 170501
San Francisco, CA 94117
BY THE TIME WE GET TO COLORADO: Vinyl $8...CS $8...CD $8

particularly ambiguous times. Being out and making an issue of it is very important.

How do you see the future of gay pop music? More queer punk music, more queer rock'n'roll as younger generations of queers get their chance to listen to music that they can relate to. Disco and Hi-NRG have no meaning to queer punks and young people.

TURTLE CREEK CHORALE: FROM THE HEART (LIVE) (1990)

Choral. The Turtle Creek Chorale (TCC) is a Dallas-based male chorus under the direction of *Dr. Timothy Seelig.* Membership in the TCC currently stands at 200 singing members. The repetoire of TCC can best be described as eclectic, drawing on everything from *Bach* to Broadway and both sacred and secular works. In 1993, the Chorale made their *Carnegie Hall* debut. They have also been the focus of the *PBS* special "After Goodbye: An AIDS Story," chronicling the stages of loss and grief recovery from AIDS by looking at the impact of the disease on the members, families and friends of the TCC. (The choir has lost 60 members during the past ten years.) Among other luminaries, the TCC has performed for Texas Governor *Ann Richards* and the *Queen of England.* This chorale, with their four albums, presents very intelligent song cycle selections. This disc contains love songs, but the chorale also has a Christmas disc, an AIDS benefit disc, and a disc featuring the work of American composers. For choral music lovers, Turtle Creek is heaven. Each disc is stuffed with over an hour's worth of song. *From The Heart* was voted "Best Choral Recording of 1990" by the readers of the national publication *CHORUS.* Like they say, the turtle only makes progress when he sticks his neck out. Stand-outs on this gorgeous disc include: "Not While I'm Around" (*Sondheim*), "Pie Jesu" (*Webber*), and "Bring Him Home" (*Boublil*).

TURTLE CREEK CHORALE: PEACE (1991)

Choral/holiday A gorgeous feast of choral music, which includes holiday favorites "The First Noel," "White Christmas," "O Holy Night," "What Child Is This?" and "Ave Maria."

TURTLE CREEK CHORALE: TESTAMENT (1992)

Choral. TCC rises to new heights of accomplished, dramatic, downright thrilling sound with punchy orchestral brilliance, all derived from a new sound process called High Definition. Joined by the *Dallas Wind Symphony*, the combination of chorus and orchestra jump off the disc, and it truly feels as if the performance is taking place in your living room. A unique listening experience, this is big audio dynamite. Focusing on the music of five 20th century American composers, *Ron Nelson, Howard Hanson, Randall Thompson, Aaron Copland* and *Leonard Bernstein, Testament* is a lesson in American history that will revive old-fashioned patriotism.

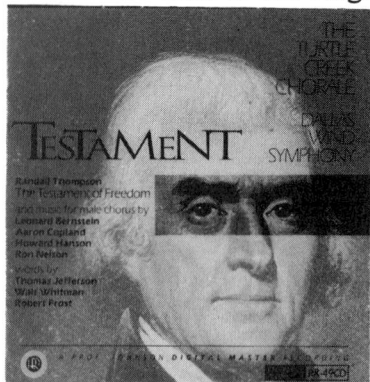

TURTLE CREEK CHORALE: WHEN WE NO LONGER TOUCH (1993)

Chorale. A transformative work of raw beauty, and a breakthrough in choral recordings, this original piece addresses the stages of grief recovery (Denial, Isolation, Anger, Bargaining, Depression, Acceptance and Hope), and benefits AmFAR. This is an incredibly moving work that is a testament to the strength and resilience of the human heart and soul, and it is based on *Peter McWilliams'* poems from the book *How To Survive The Loss Of Love.* Its blending of wit and sorrow make it a poignant, near-flawless tribute to lost love.

Dr. Seelig, describe the depth of your involvement in gay music. My own involvement in music includes being both a solo performer as well as conducting the TCC and the predominantly lesbian chorus, *The Women's Chorus of Dallas.*

Who are some of your personal artistic influences? My influences go all the way from *Dietrich Fischer Diskau* as a singer to *Robert Shaw* as a conductor to *The Flirtations* (see listing) as a singing group, and the other gay and lesbian choruses who are helping to mold the movement into a tremendous force.

What has been the impact of music on your life? Music is my life. It fills every corner. There is no doubt in my mind that music is *the* healing force in our world today...it bridges the gap between estranged children and

---

> **Turtle Creek Chorale**
> PO Box 190806
> Dallas, TX 75219-0806
> *FROM THE HEART:* CS $13...CD $18
> *PEACE:* CS $13...CD $18
> *TESTAMENT:* CS $13...CD $18
> *WHEN WE NO LONGER TOUCH:* CS $13...CD $18

parents...between diverse cultures who find no other common ground...it lifts the spirits of those sick and suffering like no other medicine can do.

Why have you chosen to do gay music? I have had careers as an opera singer in the U.S. and abroad, I have taught in a Baptist University for nine years, been a minister in one of the world's largest Baptist churches...but there is no fulfillment like that of joining gay men and lesbians together through music. There is an absolute honesty about coming together, fully knowing who we are as individuals, and sacrificing that for the good of the whole.

What is your vision of gay music? Gay music is at the birth stage, entering its very first stage of learning to walk. When we finally begin to run...watch out!

VARIOUS: A FAMILY OF FRIENDS - WOMEN'S MUSIC SAMPLER (1993)

Pop/rock/folk. The talented all-star line-up of contributors on this disc is staggering: it features some of the best of the best practitioners of New Women's Music. A solid introduction for the curious; a treat for the converted. *Jamie Anderson* has a track, as well as *Joan Armatrading* sound-alike *Pam Hall*, and veteran *Alix Dobkin* (see listing). *Sue Fink* contributes a track ("The Kind of Woman I Am") that sets this disc on its ear! *Venus Envy* (see listing) offers one of their very best originals, "Myth In Genesis," *Leah Zicari* (see listing) supplies a hearty instrumental track, *Yer Girlfriend* does "Lez-B-Bop," and I'm only scratching the surface here. If you want to explore what's new in Women's Music, this is an amazing journey of discovery. "A Family A Friends," specially written and recorded for this project, features a chorus of eighteen women, including *Margie Adam* (see listing), *Dakota, Tret Fure, Susan Herrick, Deidre McCalla* and *Cris Williamson*, among other luminaries. Proceeds from the title cut are being donated to organizations that support our community. This is hopefully the first in a long series of compelling compilations to come from *Tsunami Records*! With a stimulating variety of styles and arrangements, this is a musical feast; a Women's Music festival in your living room!

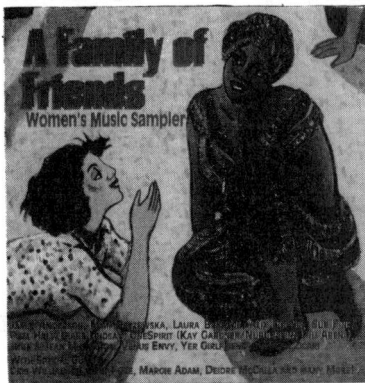

Why have you gone the gay music road as opposed to pursuing a mainstream career? Tsunami Record's JAMIE ANDERSON: I want to be honest! I'm a lesbian, so I'm

> **Tsunami Records**
> Dept. GLM
> PO Box 42282
> Tuscon, AZ 85733
> *A FAMILY OF FRIENDS*: CS $12... CD $17

going to say that in my music! And music has been one of the single most important things in my life and can be a powerful force in all people's lives because it can facilitate positive change.

What is your vision of gay music? I want gay and lesbian music to become more prominent. Queer music has a good future: as our visibility as gays and lesbians increases, so will our music.

VENUS ENVY: UNARMED AND DANGEROUS (1990)

Pop/rock vocal group. Venus Envy is a wacky, zany, original, off-the-wall, politically charged, funky feminist foursome. Their off-beat humor, effortless vocals and eclectic musical style have made them a favorite in hip, irreverent circles. An all-star project featuring *Laura Love* (see listing), *Lisa Koch* (see

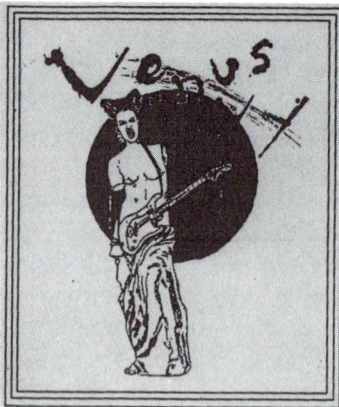

listing), *Linda Shierman,* and *Linda Severt,* their short, sharp debut release offers classics like "Venus," "Under The Boardwalk," and "Thank You For Lettinmebemyselfagain" reworked a la lesbian. The rhythmically upbeat six-song cassette has a gritty garage sound, and features some cleverly captivating rewrites of oldies. This album premiered *Love's* "Nelson" and *Koch's* "Beaver Cleaver Fever," both of which receive full production treatment on their solo albums (see listings). These two young women used Venus Envy as a jumping-off point for their stunning solo careers in gay music.

VENUS ENVY: I'LL BE A HOMO FOR CHRISTMAS (1991)

Parody/holiday. A queer take on holiday classics, this album became an instant underground classic and runaway hit upon its release. But, the explosive talent in this group was too much to be contained after their 1991 holiday recording, and the girls split to pursue solo careers. (*Laura Love* and *Lisa Koch* have top

> **Venus Envy**
> PO Box 19501
> Seattle, WA 98109
> *UNARMED AND DANGEROUS*: CS $9.99
> *I'LL BE A HOMO FOR CHRISTMAS*: CS $12

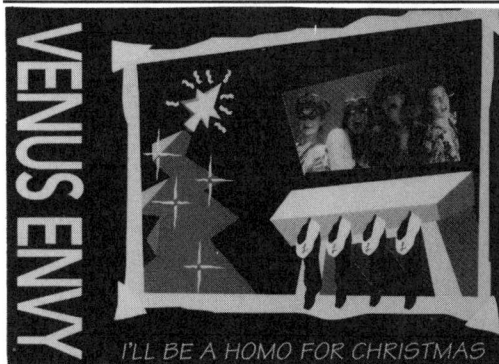

VENUS ENVY

I'LL BE A HOMO FOR CHRISTMAS

gay albums on the charts!) But...they left us laughing! *Homo* sells year round thanks to the heartwarming charm of "Rhonda The Lesbo Reindeer," "Silent Dyke," "Oh Little Town of Michigan," and of course the tender, "I Hate The Holidays." Take Venus Envy homo for the holidays. The tape is dedicated to wimmin, womons, wymym and men, and everyone whose name begins with an "L" and ends with an "A." (Venus Envy is comprised of a Lisa, a Laura and two Linda's).

How did you come to write and records a Christmas parody album in July?
There just isn't enough weird Christmas music. We did it as yet another way of broadening gay and lesbian visibility. You can reach a lot more people through humor. As they're laughing, they receive a larger message through osmosis. It just sort of seeps in.

LAURA WETZLER: A WORLD OF JEWISH FOLK MUSIC (1992)

Folk/Ethnic. Wetzler's premier release is a beautiful, spirited collection of fifteen songs in three Jewish languages, plus Wetzler's wonderful original, "Smoke of the Battle." Singing in Yiddish, Hebrew and Ladino, she reveals a voice with the range, passion and flexibility of *Kate Bush*. The result is a remarkable listening experience, even if you don't understand the language.

Laura Wetzler

LAURA WETZLER: THE JESSE HELMS SAMPLER (1993)

Folk. Singer-songwriter Laura Wetzler burst onto the alternative music scene with her independent cult hit, "Jesse Helms Has Made A Radical Out Of Me," an anti-censorship single which has played on radio stations across the U.S. and Canada. Her adaptation and setting of *Maya Angelou*'s poem "Nobody's Going To Make It Out Here Alone" was heard all over New York City in the wake of the disturbances in Crown Heights and L.A. Needless to say, Wetzler has a sharp eye for social and political commentary. Her hilarious satire bites with the sting of wickedly informed humor. She's an eclectic urban folkie

LAURA WETZLER

Jesse Helms Has Made a Radical Out of Me

whose five-song sampler includes her most well-known piece, "Jesse Helms Has Made A Radical Out Of Me," as well as the au courant "Lesbian Chic" ("There were lesbians before lesbians were chic / we don't need permission from *20/20* or *Newsweek*"), and two moving ballads, "Why Do I Run" (which features amazing fiddle work!) and "Nobody's Going To Make It Out Here Alone." Wetzler's is a compelling voice, beautiful, clear and soaring, which will hopefully be speaking out for years to come.

Why have you chosen a career as an out lesbian musician, and what's it like being an out lesbian performer? I am insatiably curious about everything, so it's a good life for me. I love it. I sing and write in different styles and get involved in a variety of projects. Being a working musician, I sing for all kinds of audiences. I believe that good singing and writing that comes from the heart can transcend lines of differences. I'm out because I don't want to waste myself in hiding. Every human experience can shape and inspire; I want to use it all and celebrate it all.

What do you think is the future of gay pop music? My hope is that the commercial music business would become more open-minded. The world is wide and made fascinating and beautiful with every different voice. There is room for all of us.

> **Laura Wetzler**
> Nervy Girl Productions
> 557 Union Street
> Brooklyn, NY 11215
> *THE JESSE HELMS SAMPLER*: CS $6
> *A WORLD OF JEWISH FOLK MUSIC*: CS $11

WINDY CITY GAY CHORUS: MOSTLY LOVE (1991)

Choral. This chorus is a stunning example of the revival of male choral singing in North America. Windy City Gay Chorus' precision, flexibility of style, warmth of color, well-balanced tone, firm diction, and meticulous attention to detail add up to what some have termed the finest male chorus in the country. Accessible and well-paced, this tape could convert even the most resolute

> **Windy City Performing Arts**
> 3023 N. Clark #329
> Chicago, IL 60657
> *MOSTLY LOVE*: CS $12
> *DON WE NOW*: CS $12...CD $17

disparagers of choral music. The work charms, lulls and ultimately seduces. What really works here is the blending of obscure and familiar material: "The Great Peace March" (*Holly Near*), "What'll I Do?" (*Irving Berlin*), and "Where Is Love?" (*Lionel Bart*) being among the familiar. Give this tape to someone you love. The beauty of the chorus washes over you in waves upon waves of gorgeous sound. WCGC is now into its second decade of music making. They have won first place in the *Great American Choral Festival*, and have received grants based on musical excellence from the *National Endowment for the Arts*, *The Illinois Arts Council* and *ChorusAmerica*.

WINDY CITY GAY CHORUS: DON WE NOW... (1992)

Choral/Christmas. One of the founders of the gay choral movement in America presents tasty selections of Christmas favorites, including: "Deck The Halls," "Silent Night," and "White Christmas." There's something about the Windy City Gay Chorus that makes the listening experience intimate as well as grandly entertaining. A great stocking-stuffer, this tape will get you a-wassailing.

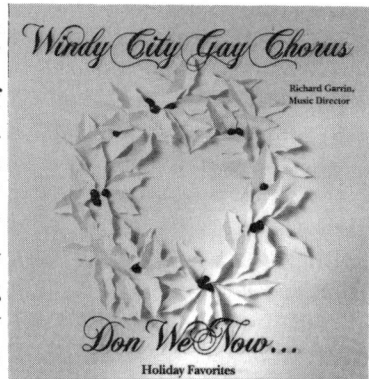

WORM: WORM (1992)

Synth/pop and folk. Worm is a one-of-a-kind vocal/songwriting duo of twins: a gay brother and a lesbian sister! On their debut release, they tap an analog synth production sound that hearkens back to *Yaz* and early *Eurythmics*. The duo blends beautifully balanced harmonies as well as vocal solos that brother and sister trade off. With honesty, clarity and poppy melodic hooks, the Seattle siblings grapple with issues of acceptance, same-sex relationships, justice, coming out, freedom, equal rights and world peace. Best tracks here are "Woman Of The Third Wave" and "Gay Nineties." The wonderful acoustic guitar work of sister Janie is showcased on her contributions while keyboardist

Jamie explores synth-pop grooves on his compositions, and that's what I like

best about this release: it is the ultimate in inclusion. The gay male and lesbian/feminist viewpoints exist side by side as well as merge, and this formula is what it's all about: coming together as brothers and sisters.
How do you approach being a gay artist?
JIMMY: I write about what I feel. Part of what I feel comes from my experience as a gay man. What I feel also comes from my experiences as a son, a brother, a partner, a lover. Being an out gay performer allows me to write about everything I am.

What does music mean to you? JANIE: Music is a beautiful tool that speaks to anyone with a heartbeat. That inherent ability to relate stirs emotions, shapes thoughts and dreams, triggers memories...music is a fun way of discovering these and other parts of ourselves in knowing who we are at any moment in time.

Why did you want to be an out gay musician?
JIMMY: Growing up in rural Arkansas, I was not exposed to positive gay role models. In 1973, I watched my gay brother ingest a permanently mind altering drug to, in part, deal with his sexuality. Seven years and many mental institutions later, he killed

> **WORM**
> 2103 Harrison NW
> Suite 2414
> Olympia, WA 98502
> *WORM*: CS $12

himself. I am so tired of all our creative energy being expended to pacify mainstream America while gay and lesbian youth continue to kill and abuse themselves because they feel isolated and alone. I consider it a matter of life and death that gay and lesbian artists present life from our perspective.

What is your vision of gay music? JANIE: I believe that gay pop will follow its predecessors into mainstream. The music industry always seems to be looking for something new. Consumers always seem to be looking for something familiar. Gay pop music is uniquely both of these. Lesbian and gay issues have become more prominent. Though many people still see us as oddities, our music sings to the same basic human emotions of love, fear, pride, loss, etc. At the emotional level at which music inspires us, I think it will be easy for most folks to see our similarities.

Y'ALL: AN EVENING OF STORIES & SONGS (1993)

White trash country gospel. As a lowbrow, southern fried, trailer park *Simon & Garfunkel*, it is astonishing how well these two men illumine the gay experience. It is really surprising that they have gotten overwhelming positive and downright affectionate coverage for their stage act (performed by the six foot three inch Jay Byrd in his lucky green dress, and shirtless Steven Cheslik-DeMeyer in beat-up overalls) in *both* the gay *and* straight media. Their sound is a mix of rural Americana: gospel, country/western and bluegrass music performed *Hee-Haw* style with superb harmonizing. James Dean Jay Byrd is the son of a tent revivalist from Okey-Dokey, Texas and the nephew of a trailerhome salesman/crossdresser. His pardner Steven is a former corn farmer from Corn Flake, Indiana, and the seventeenth child of former Catholics. "I Am the Queen Of The Rodeo" and "Man Who's Not In My Family Tree" (about grandpa's boyfriend) are knee-slappin' stand-outs in these homespun tales of rural gay life. Steven plays guitar and ukulele while Jay plays a variety of home-made instruments like a jar of beans, a kazoo, and a washboard and whisk. All of Y'ALL's songs are heartfelt originals, from lonely trail-riding tunes, to everybody-join-in hillbilly ditties, to classic-styled gospel numbers. Their magic is that these low-rent *Smothers Brothers* can spin out a clownish song about three outcast lesbians who commit suicide after giving a bad bouffant, and romanticize down-home living while at the same time revealing its bizarre peculiarities.

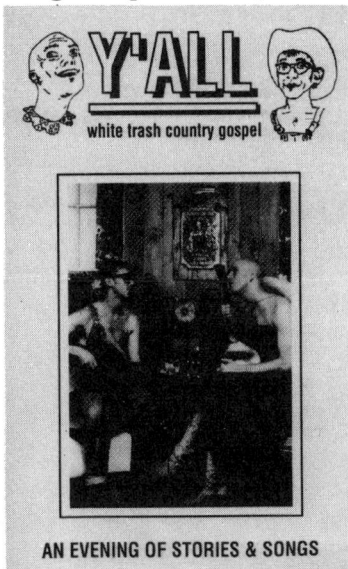

white trash country gospel

AN EVENING OF STORIES & SONGS

Y'ALL white trash country gospel
235 E. 10th Street, Studio G
New York, NY 10003-7666
Hotline: (212) 473-YALL
AN EVENING OF STORIES & SONGS: CS $11

How do you define gay music? Gay music is music made by gay and lesbian people that speaks of their experience as gay and lesbian people. We believe that music is a basic part of everyone's lives. It touches people's souls.

Why have you chosen to do gay music? We never chose to be out per se. I guess the idea of concealing aspects of our lives as important and interesting and full of subject matter for songs as our sexuality and our relationship didn't even occur to us. People have told us that we could really make it big if we weren't out. But we see our openness as so central to the whole idea of Y'ALL, our message, our mission, that we would be nothing if we were closeted. We can't even imagine what that would be like. And we still believe that our message is universal enough that we don't have to see our career as marginal and limited. So far, our experience with gay, straight and mixed audiences have gotten equally positive responses. We're striving to be America's favorite gay couple.

Look into the future... We look forward to a time when the categories like gay music aren't necessary. We see what we do as an important part of creating that world.

LEAH ZICARI: WOULDN'T THAT BE FUN? (1990)

Pop/folk/rock. Wouldn't That Be Fun? is an important work of major proportions by an amazingly gifted artist who is one of those rare barometers of the community. Zicari lets you into those terrifying corners of our common psyche, the shadows where the shame hides alongside lurking age-old fears. By being brazenly self-revealing in the confessional style of *Joni Mitchell*, Zicari allows us to tend our own wounds, face our own quirks, fears, dreams, nightmares, rational lies, and ultimately, our truth. This tape careens from comic doo-wop ("What Kind of Self-Respecting Lezzie Am I?"), to defiant battle cries of outrage ("Laws"), to the gospel anthem of our community, ("Glory, Glory," to the tune of "The Battle Hymn of The Republic.") In "Glory, Glory," the words are changed to "Glory, glory, I'm a lesbian / Glory, glory, I'm a gay man / Glory, glory, I'm a homosexual / I am truth marching on." Strong affirmations of our common humanity are here, as well as visits from *The Bionic Woman, Charlie's Angels* and *Martina* in cameo lyrical appearances. Zicari's brilliance is that she encompasses the full breadth of the gay/lesbian experience and writes cleverly and passionately enough to communicate the message as well as her spunky personality. Zicari utilizes her Master's Degree in classical guitar with flourish here, highlighted by an instrumental piece of sophisticated jazz virtuosity called "Special Friends and Computers." She has appeared in *Tom Wilson Weinberg's Ten Percent Review* and was voted Favorite New Performer in the 1991 and 1992 *Hotwire* Reader's Choice Awards. Her work can also be heard on the compilation *A Family of Friends* (see listing) and on

the *1993 March on Washington's Pride Anthem,* which she also conducted. With stark tenderness, sophisticated acoustic jazz/folk arrangements, and the confidence to tackle subjects like religious patriarchy and the desperation of growing up lesbian, this is a substantial and provocative work. **Describe your music and tell me why you are an out gay musician.** My music is outrageous queer music, poignant ballads, clever and in-your-face and unapologetic. Being an out performer is uniquely fulfilling because I believe I am helping to create our own culture.

> **Gender Bender Music**
> PO Box 164
> Buffalo, NY 14207
> *WOULDN'T THAT BE FUN?* CS $12

How has music impacted your life, and how do you hope your music will impact other people's lives? Music hasn't impact my life; it *is* my life. I would not exist without it. I hope my music allows gays and lesbians *and* non-gays to view queers in an honest, humorous and proud way. Non-gays can be exposed to our culture in a non-threatening way, and gays can feel proud of who we are.

What is your vision of gay music? I think that once being queer is trendy and record execs get wind of the huge queer market and talent pool, that they'll be snapping us up and signing us to record deals (and taking total credit for discovering us)!

REJOURCEJ: GAY & LEJBIAN MUJIC
CULTURE/ENTERTAINMENT/INFORMATION

HOT WIRE MAGAZINE: The Journal of Women's Music & Culture
5210 N. Wayne
Chicago, IL 60640
(312) 769-9009
Great articles, profiles, interviews, and soundsheets make this magazine a must-have. It is published three times a year, is well-written, entertaining, features Reader's Choice Awards, and great classifieds! $17/year.

WOMEN'S MUSIC PLUS: Directory of Resources in Women's Culture
Yearly directory. Call for price. Published by *Hot Wire* (see listing above).
This invaluable directory contains listings of performers, agents, festivals, producers, photographers, radio shows, libraries and archives, periodicals, bookstores, organizations, etc. Absolutely incredible information resource.

LADYSLIPPER CATALOG & RESOURCE GUIDE
(800) 634-6044
The most complete catalog of recordings by women (straight and lesbian). There is also a smattering of recordings listed in the "Mehn's Music" section. Call for information.

OUTcast PRODUCTIONS
38-11 Ditmars Boulevard, Suite 234
Astoria, NY 11105
(718) 728-4794
Brave new music distribution company for lesbian and gay musicians, and women in rock. Great catalog available! $5.00.

SHE'S A REBEL; Gillian G. Gaar; Seal Press (1992)
This is by far the best history of women in rock and roll ever written. The book contains lengthy sections on the history of Women's Music, and covers topics such as lesbianism, feminism, festivals, etc.

THE VINYL CLOSET; Boze Hadleigh; Los Hombres Press (1991); $9.95
Hadleigh's book is an entertaining and fun romp through the long history of gays in music. The majority of the contemporary references deal with British artists, and several interviewees remain annoyingly anonymous, but from a historical perspective this is an essential work.

MUSICA FEMINA REPORT
(503) 233-1206
As part of their ongoing research into music by women composers, Janna MacAuslan of *Musica Femina* has compiled and distributes a catalog which lists works by women for guitar, including both solos and other instruments and voice. Call for details.

OPTION MAGAZINE
1522-B Cloverfield Blvd.
Santa Monica, CA 90404
Bi-monthly, $15.95 a year (six issues)
Option is the most open-minded guide to alternative music today. The articles, listings and interviews are intelligent and informed, and the magazine gives fair and enthusiastic coverage to gay and lesbian bands and artists.

ALL MUSIC GUIDE; Erlewine & Bultman, editors; Miller Freeman, Inc.
A huge reference of over 1,100 pages, the All Music Guide reviews thousands of albums in all types of music styles, including a short section on Women's Music and an intelligent (but not very complete) survey of Gay Music written by Tom Wilson Weinberg *(Ten Percent Review)*. $19.95.

GAYELLOW PAGES
Box 292, Village Station
New York, NY 10014
(212) 674-0120—Call for prices.
This phenomenal reference to our community can put you in touch with clubs, performers, bookstores that sell gay and lesbian music, magazines and newspapers, broadcast media, and many other entertainment related services. They produce a national edition as well as a number of regional editions.

NETWORK Q
3215-A Central Avenue NE
Albuquerque, NM 87106
A video magazine available by subscription, Network Q specializes in features about art and culture, and has given extensive coverage to queer musicians, comedians, authors and performance artists. Call (800) 368-0638 for rates.

PARTY TALK (Cable Access) and IN THE LIFE (Public Television)
Consult your local cable and public television guides. At press time, there are a handful of explicitly gay programs popping up that regularly feature musical entertainment. Pending satellite syndication will make the new cable programs available to a much larger national audience.

Editor's Picks: TOP GAY ALBUMS

NO.	ARTIST	ALBUM TITLE
1	DOUG STEVENS & THE OUTBAND	OUT IN THE COUNTRY
2	DOS FALLOPIA	MY BREASTS ARE OUT OF CONTROL
3	THE FLIRTATIONS	LIVE: OUT ON THE ROAD
4	LISA KOCH	COLORBLIND BLUES
5	ROMANOVSKY & PHILLIPS	BE POLITICAL, NOT POLITE
6	ALIX DOBKIN	LOVE & POLITICS: A 30 YEAR SAGA
7	MICHAEL CALLEN	PURPLE HEART
8	DAN MARTIN & MICHAEL BIELLO	HUMAN BEING
9	LAURA LOVE	PANGAEA
10	PUSSY TOURETTE	PUSSY TOURETTE IN HI-FI
11	VARIOUS	A FAMILY OF FRIENDS
12	PHIDEAUX	"FRICTION"
13	RUS McCOY	THE ACE SESSIONS
14	MARGIE ADAM	ANOTHER PLACE
15	RON ROMANOVSKY	HOPEFUL ROMANTIC
16	TOM McCORMACK	ROSE COLORED GLASSES
17	BILL McKINLEY	EVERYTHING POSSIBLE
18	MARSHA STEVENS	I STILL HAVE A DREAM
19	THE RHYTHM METHOD	THE RHYTHM METHOD
20	QUEER CONSCIENCE	BACK TO THE OTHER WORLD?
21	JOSEPH VICTOR SIEGER	SELF-PORTRAIT, 1993
22	LYNN LAVNER	BUTCH FATALE
23	JAN TILLEY	SCARLET LETTER
24	TOMMIE SAELI	HELLO
25	KEITH CHRISTOPHER	KEITH CHRISTOPHER

HOW TO BUILD A GAY MUSIC COLLECTION

With the wealth of all the great new gay and lesbian music available to you, where do you start when you want to build a collection of gay music? The best place to start is by listening to the Gay Music Sampler and ordering the albums of the artists that catch your ear.

As far as must-have's, they include: Michael Callen's *Purple Heart*. This is the Gay Music Hall of Fame All-Time Winner. There has never been a more perfect album of gay music conceived, performed or produced. You should also have at least one Romanovsky & Phillips album in your collection. R&P are gay music pioneers who produce smooth pop albums in a variety of styles, with a consistent emphasis on gay issues and themes. And, whether you are a rabid Women's Music fan or you just need an introduction to the genre, *A Family Of Friends (The Women's Music Sampler)* is a critical addition to your collection for the sheer variety of artists and wealth of musicians on the disc.

Women's Music foremothers Alix Dobkin and Margie Adam should certainly be represented in your collection. Dobkin's latest release is a 30-year retrospective that will catch you up with this amazing pioneer. Margie Adam's latest release (*Another Place*) is a summation of a stellar career, and a gorgeous piece of work.

The New Women in Gay Pop Music are producing some of the most exciting albums on the contemporary scene. Lisa Koch, Laura Love, Amy Fix, and others have spectacular material available.

Gay music pioneers The Flirtations should certainly be represented. For the campy and moving experience of this group live, check out *Live On The Road*. The late Joe Bracco has a stunning tape available (*True To Myself*), featuring his New York-flavored New Wave and ballads. The album is a jaw-dropper.

It is certainly recommended that you get a hold of the #1 and #2 Gay Albums: *Out In The Country* by Doug Stevens & The Outband, and *My Breasts Are Out Of Control* by Dos Fallopia. You also cannot go wrong with any of the albums listed on the Top 25 Gay Albums Chart.

From there, you might want to explore genres that are your personal favorites. In cabaret, for example, you could choose D.C. Anderson, Bill McKinley, or Dan Martin. In Alternative Rock, there are many choices, including Phideaux, Tommie Saeli, and Rick Robertson. In Contemporary Christian music you have the choice of David & Jane, Marsha Stevens, Joe Mack Boyd and others. There are many exciting new discoveries ahead for you. And don't forget to share this music with your friends and lovers! There's no greater gift than the gift of gay music.

"Have you got a friend for me?"